Footfalls in Memory

ALSO BY TERRY WAITE

Taken on Trust

Terry Waite

Footfalls in Memory

REFLECTIONS FROM

SOLITUDE

Footfalls echo in the memory
Down the passage which we did not take
Towards the door we never opened
Into the rose-garden. My words echo
Thus in your mind.

T.S. Eliot
'Burnt Norton', *The Four Quartets*

I have sought for rest everywhere
But I have found it nowhere except in a corner with a book

Thomas à Kempis

CORONET BOOKS
Hodder and Stoughton

British Library Cataloguing in Publication Data
A record for this book is available from the British Library

ISBN 0 340 66922 5

Typeset by Hewer Text Composition Services, Edinburgh
Printed and bound in Great Britain by
Cox & Wyman Ltd, Reading, Berks

Hodder and Stoughton Ltd
A Division of Hodder Headline PLC
338 Euston Road
London NW1 3BH

THIS COLLECTION IS DEDICATED TO THE
MANY THOUSANDS OF MEN, WOMEN
AND CHILDREN THROUGHOUT THE
WORLD WHO REMEMBERED THE BEIRUT
HOSTAGES AND TO THOSE WHO WROTE
TO ME AND MY FAMILY ON MY RELEASE

THANK YOU

ACKNOWLEDGMENTS

Many people have assisted me with this book and I am grateful to them for their support and friendship. Eric Major from Hodder and Stoughton encouraged me to write it and was always available to share his considerable knowledge. Teresa de Bertodano was the most unobtrusive and skilful of editors. Harry Cory-Wright took the photographs for the cover a mile or so from our house in Suffolk. Pete Viccars contributed the woodcuts. Lavinia Barnes and Mark Lucas provided support without which I would have been quite lost. Tom Sutherland took the trouble to send me a list of all the books he could remember reading in captivity and I am grateful to him. Barbara Ellis has my thanks for her competent copy-editing, and proof-reading. Finally, my gratitude to Frances my wife for her patience and understanding. Of course, I alone take responsibility for any shortcomings in the book.

INTRODUCTION

PEOPLE frequently ask me what it was that I missed most during the years spent in solitary confinement. My answer is clear. Apart from the obvious – family, friends and freedom – I missed books. I pleaded with the guards to bring me books and for the first year or so they ignored my requests. I was forced to depend upon memory and travelled back across the years to recall books I had read during my life. I made a list in my mind of those I had read during childhood. In my imagination I travelled to my study in London and gazed at the volumes on the shelves. I even dreamt about books. One night I dreamt that I was at home gazing at the volumes around me. Just as I was about to take one down I felt something tug at my ankle and awoke. I had turned in my sleep and the chain securing my foot to the wall had pulled and disturbed my dream. I can still feel the disappointment at being denied the pleasure of reading.

After a year or so the guards made an effort to bring me books, but they faced some difficulties. First, they had to be careful in obtaining them; if they had been seen buying large quantities of English books they might have drawn unwelcome attention to themselves. Second, as most of them had a limited understanding of English they did not know what they were bringing. One day, after much pleading on my part because it had been so long since the last book, a friendly guard said that he would bring me something to read. He tapped on the door of my cell: the signal to me to fasten my blindfold. The guard came into the room and dropped a book on the floor. As he left I quickly removed the covering from my eyes. When I picked up the precious volume I laughed out loud at the title. *Great Escapes* by Eric Williams, a book of stories detailing escapes from prison camps in World War II.

The American hostage, Terry Anderson, requested large books and received *Diseases of the Middle Ear*. He claims to have read it from cover to cover.

As the years went by books began to trickle through. Because I had no reading glasses with me I was provided with a tiny magnifying glass which would enlarge one word at a time. Later this was changed for a larger glass which made reading easier. Whenever I received a book I would count the number of pages and work out how many words it contained. I knew exactly how long it would take me to finish it and as I am a fast reader I had to discipline myself to read slowly.

To be alone with a book was one of the most precious gifts I received during those long solitary years. I read with a degree of concentration that I had not experienced since childhood. Whenever biographical details were given I was delighted and as I read I attempted to enter into the mind of the author. Books appeared to which I would not have given a second thought in the outside world. At one point I was given a large selection of crime fiction and discovered the excellent writers in that genre. All types of books eventually arrived. The ubiquitous Dr Spock made a brief call followed by a textbook on breast feeding! Despite my protests about these two, I was told to read them and be thankful that I had been given anything at all.

On my release in 1991 I was elected Fellow Commoner at Trinity Hall, Cambridge, and settled down to put on paper the book I had written in my head during captivity: *Taken on Trust*. Every Tuesday and Thursday I would go to the market square in Cambridge and sort through the volumes on the second-hand book-stall. As soon as I came across a title I had read in Beirut I bought it to add to my collection.

Footfalls in Memory is the record of a journey made in the company of books. It brings together selections from some of the volumes I had been given by my guards and excerpts from others I held in memory when I had nothing to read. It also includes selections from books I wished I had had with me during those days, beginning with some of those I remembered from my earliest years and concluding with a reflection on childhood. In between, there is a very broad range of material covering many different experiences. *Footfalls in Memory* is also the record of an exploration into the self – a journey towards the centre.

Solitary confinement taught me anew the delight and value of books. I am happy to share something of that with the readers of this collection and I hope that these pages will bring the reader as much satisfaction as the books I have chosen have brought to me.

Terry Waite
Suffolk, 1995

ALMOST as soon as I was captured I began to tread the long corridor of memory. I travelled back across the years to a childhood lived in the threadbare tatters of post-war Britain. In the first weeks of solitude it was as though I had become as a child. Vulnerable, questioning, anxious, demanding, angry, I was denied companionship and all freedom except that of wandering at will in my imagination. As my early requests for books went unheeded, I started to make a list of all those I could remember from childhood. In my insecurity, I began to look back in an attempt to find a safe place.

One of the first books I brought to mind was by G. Bramwell Evens, better known as Romany of the BBC. Evens was born into a true gypsy family and although he became a Methodist minister he never lost the urge to wander. Each year he would set out in his wooden caravan,

Vardo as he called it, and travel through the north of England. His programmes, broadcast on the BBC *Children's Hour*, introduced thousands of young people to the wonders of nature. It might be said that Romany was the first of a long line of radio naturalists. Today, his caravan is in Wilmslow, Cheshire, and is open to the public at certain times of the year. There is also a small memorial to his faithful dog Raq. Years later we gave our own springer spaniel the same name.

Only recently I discovered a remote but curious link with Romany; the lady who typed his manuscripts for publication had been a bridesmaid at my parents' wedding.

I have chosen a short passage from *A Romany in the Fields*, as the simple descriptions remind me of the days I spent playing on a farmyard in rural Cheshire. I thought of those days as I lay on a cold stone floor, chained, blindfolded and denied my freedom.

Of all the many recreations which I enjoy, I believe that 'pottering about' holds first place in my affections. It is the art of loitering – not with intent to commit a felony, but in order to see the most in that small radius of territory which lies within a few yards of one's eyes. I feel I have a great deal in common with him who said, 'The eyes of a fool are in the ends of the earth.'

There are many such places which are favourites of mine. I delight to linger wherever there is the sound of running water. How can I do justice to the pleasure which is more akin to a spell which steals over me as I rest on some mossy bank listening to the breeze as it rustles the tops of a field of oats, barley, or wheat?

But, of all the places which lure me to stay, the farmyard has a supreme fascination.

To begin with, I love its varied smells and scents. Even those which are not usually associated with lavender or attar of roses give me a pleasure that I cannot describe. I look over the low walls of the sty, and what I should describe as offensive were it to greet me in the city I find a certain pleasure in now that I am in rural surroundings.

Of course, if the inhabitant be an old sow, and running round her be a litter of youngsters, then the picture is complete. I wait for her to give a grunt of interrogation as she sees my face peering at her. I answer her politely, quietly, soothingly, and she at once imparts a slightly different tone to her next effort. It is less harsh, less suspicious. She accepts me as a well-wisher, and, all fears having departed, she rolls over on to her side. Immediately there is a rush amongst the young life that is ever hungry, to secure, so to speak, the best seats.

What a magnificent sight of anxious motherhood is it to see those rooting, pushful, vigorous piglets getting a morning meal! How careful is she lest her ponderous weight crush one of those silken-haired, pink delights! How they squeak out their woe and indignation until the warm stream of nutrition trickles down their outstretched throats, and until, at last, nothing can be heard save the mother's hard breathing and an occasional squeal of protest from some youngster whom another tries to displace!

Then at the end of the feeding crowd I look for the 'runt' or the 'reckling'. It is the weakest of the lot. You can always spot him.

There he is, and he must take his chance with the strongest. His little legs are not so sturdy as those of his brothers and sisters – you can see his ribs pressing out from his spare body. He takes what is left after all the others have had their fill. Youth for him is going to be a struggle. Perhaps he will survive – perhaps not. But, with all her motherhood, there is no hint that the old sow has any particular sympathy for little 'runt'. If he lives, he lives.

But in human society it is the 'reckling' to which we pay special attention. It is the 'reckling' which survives and lives, perchance, to pass on its weakness to others, who may in their turn be 'recklings' too. In Nature the weakest go to the wall. In human nature the weakest receive the strength of the strong – what a gulf really separates the two kingdoms!

G. Bramwell Evens
A Romany in the Fields

MANY of the books I have saved from childhood are cheaply printed and stamped, 'Book Production. War Economy Standard'. Colour illustrations were largely unknown except perhaps for a colourful dust jacket. One book I remembered was *William* because it retained its original red cover. Richmal Crompton delighted my generation with dozens of her William stories. On one of the inside pages twenty-nine different titles are listed; the author must have grown somewhat weary of writing about William and the Outlaws. The back cover of my book introduces 'Jimmy' with the words, 'If you like William, you'll like Jimmy, Richmal Crompton's new boy hero.' Unlike William, who has survived to entertain the children of today, Jimmy has disappeared.

In company with Romany, William was also a radio hero. Books and the radio belong together as both demand an active use of the imagination. Through both it is possible to create an inner world and face issues which will have to be dealt with in later life.

Years after reading the William books I came across an interesting psychological exploration of children's literature in *The Child and the Book* by Nicholas Tucker. Here the author is discussing the particular appeal of William Brown.

On the surface, William has many attributes that children find attractive or amusing. His leadership qualities, unrestrained fantasy-life and determined rejection of adult standards of dress, etiquette and modes of speech, do give him some of the traditional appeal of the anti-establishment rebel . . . and the adults he makes look silly are just those grown-ups that sometimes sit rather heavily upon young people. But William is also a victim of his own obvious immaturity: things rarely happen as he wishes them to – often very much the reverse. This is in marked contrast to Enid Blyton adventure stories, where everything always works out well. With William, plans are usually bungled, and his audience is encouraged to see why and to laugh at the results. William's romanticism, for example, makes him the softest of touches for crooks with a good line in sob-stories, and his strong feelings for the opposite sex are made to seem ridiculous, especially when aimed at the mature young ladies that the much older Robert fancies. While physical difficulties disappear and child-heroes emerge unscathed in a Blyton novel, with William reality undermines most of his grandiose intentions, and his reception at the end of each adventure is usually not a flattering one. He will always defend his actions though, and fail to understand or learn from his mistakes – another aspect of that same egocentricity which better-behaved readers may admire for its audacity however immature it may also appear.

In this way, William can sometimes be a butt for others, as he has some of the innocence as well as the egotistic assertiveness of a much younger child. Take this passage, where he is trying to make positive overtures towards his otherwise rejecting father (although once again, the strong possibility of William's underlying aggression in all this must also be considered):

William, standing at the dining-room window and surveying the world at large, could not for the moment think of anything to do. From the window he saw the figure of his father who sat peacefully on the lawn reading a newspaper. William was not fond of his own society. He liked company of any sort. He went out to the lawn and stood by his father's chair.

'You've not got much hair on the top of your head, father,' he said pleasantly and conversationally.

There was no answer.

'I said you'd not got much hair on the top of your head,' repeated William in a louder tone.

'I heard you,' said his father coldly.

'Oh,' said William, sitting down on the ground. There was silence for a minute, then William said in friendly tones:

'I only said it again 'cause I thought you didn't hear the first time. I thought you'd have said, "Oh", or "Yes", or "No", or something if you'd heard.'

There was no answer, and again after a long silence, William spoke.

'I didn't mind you not sayin' "Oh", or "Yes", or "No",' he said, 'only that was what made me say it again, 'cause with you not sayin' it I thought you'd not heard.'

Mr Brown arose and moved his chair several feet away. William, on whom hints were wasted, followed.

'I was readin' a tale yesterday,' he said, 'about a man wot's legs got bit off by sharks – '

Mr Brown groaned.

'William', he said politely, 'pray don't
let me keep you from your friends.'
'Oh, no, that's quite all right,' said
William. 'Well – p'raps Ginger is
lookin' for me. Well, I'll finish about
the man an' the sharks after tea. You'll
be here then, won't you?'

'Please, don't trouble,' said Mr Brown
with sarcasm that was entirely lost on
his son.

'Oh, it's not a trouble,' said William
as he strolled off. 'I like talkin' to
people.'

Most of his readers, however, will understand Mr Brown's sarcasm, even if William
cannot, just as they will see the obvious
flaws in his schemes and general perception
of events. So although William's fans can
revel in the things he does, they are not at
the same time encouraged to accept him as
an idealised fantasy about themselves. In
this sense, Enid Blyton colludes with the

immaturity of her audience's response, by taking up children's most infantile fantasies at face value, while Richmal Crompton suggests that such immature daydreams never prove very effective when put into practice, however funny they may be to read about. There may not be the same quality of adventurous abandon in reading a William book, therefore, but far more opportunity for humour, something always likely when there are large gaps between a character's hopes and performance. William thus belongs to a long line of comic anti-heroes in literature who never understand quite how incompetent they are, and a young audience can feel pleasantly superior when confronted by such examples of misadventure.

Nicholas Tucker
The Child and the Book

REMEMBERING can be painful, and for much of my captivity I hardly allowed myself to think about family and friends in order to protect myself from emotions which might have got the better of me.

There were times when I thought about my wife Frances, and frequently of the times she made me laugh. When our children were small, Frances maintained a tradition, received from her own mother, of always reading stories and rhymes to them at bedtime. Much of what she read she had learnt by heart and I remembered her reciting with great spirit Hilaire Belloc's sad tale of Henry King:

HENRY KING

Who chewed bits of string and was cut off in dreadful agonies

The Chief Defect of Henry King
Was chewing little bits of String.
At last he swallowed some which tied
Itself in ugly Knots inside.

Physicians of the Utmost Fame
Were called at once; but when they came
They answered, as they took their Fees,
'There is no Cure for this Disease.
Henry will very soon be dead'
His Parents stood about his Bed
Lamenting his Untimely Death,
When Henry, with his Latest Breath,
Cried 'Oh, my Friends, be warned by me,
That Breakfast, Dinner, Lunch, and Tea
Are all the Human Frame requires . . . '
With that, the Wretched Child expires.

Hilaire Belloc
*The Penguin Book of
Comic and Curious Verse*

THERE is a bookshop in Cambridge which specialises in books for children and I frequently take a look inside. Many of the books I enjoyed years ago are still in print. Books by Arthur Ransome stand out: *Peter Duck, We didn't mean to go to Sea* and of course *Swallows and Amazons*. Dated they may be, but clearly they continue to appeal to the present generation. I recollect being totally absorbed by Ransome's books. In a note at the front of *Swallows and Amazons* the author tells us how the book grew out of his childhood memories of holidays in the English Lake District.

My first visit to Windermere was on a school trip in the early 1950s. The occasion is indelibly impressed on my mind as it was the first time I played croquet. I attempted to liven up the game by using the mallet as one would use a golf club. Unfortunately I felled a school friend who was standing behind me. I have had nothing to do with croquet since.

When *Swallows and Amazons* first appeared in 1930 critics foretold that it would become a children's classic. The following extract describes how the children prepare to set out on a voyage of adventure. I have included it, not only on account of childhood memories but because one of my ways of passing the time when I had nothing to read was to provision a boat in my imagination. Perhaps this passage had rested in my subconscious for years . . .

THE VOYAGE TO THE ISLAND

There were three sailors of Bristol City
Who took a boat and went to sea.
But first with beef and captain's biscuits
And pickled pork they loaded she.
William Thackeray

There was very little room in the *Swallow* when they had finished loading her at the little jetty by the boathouse. Under the main thwart was a big tin box with the books and writing-paper and other things that had to be kept dry, like night-clothes. In this box was also a small aneroid barometer. John had won it as a prize at school and never went anywhere without it. Underneath the forward thwart, on each side of the mast, were large biscuit tins, with bread, tea, sugar, salt, biscuits, tins of corned beef, tins of sardines, a lot of eggs, each one wrapped separately for fear of smashes, and a big seed cake. Right forward, in front of the mast, was a long coil of stout grass rope and the anchor, but it had been found by trying that there was room for the Boy Roger here in the bows as look-out man. Then there were the two groundsheets, in which were rolled up the tents, each with the rope that belonged to it. These were stowed just aft of the mast. The whole of the space that was left in the bottom of the boat was filled by two big sacks stuffed with blankets and rugs. Besides all these there were the things that could not be packed at all, but had to go loose, wedged in anyhow, things like the saucepan and frying-pan and kettle, and a big farm lantern. Then there was a basket full of mugs, plates, spoons, forks, and knives. There was no room for anything else big except the crew and there on the jetty were four great hay-bags, stuffed with hay by Mr Jackson, the farmer, which were to serve as beds and mattresses.

'We shall have to make two trips of it,' said Captain John.

'Or three,' said Mate Susan. 'Even with *Swallow* empty we shall never be able to get more than three of the haybags into her at once.'

Able-seaman Titty had an idea. 'Couldn't we get a native to bring them in a native rowing-boat?' she said.

John looked back into the boathouse at the big rowing-boat belonging to the farm. He knew, because it had been privately arranged, that mother was to pay them a visit before night to see that all was well. He knew, too, that it had been arranged that

Mr Jackson, the farmer, should row her. Mr Jackson was as good a native as anyone could wish.

Mother and nurse, carrying Vicky, were coming down the field.

John went to meet them. It was agreed that the natives would bring the haybags in a rowing-boat.

'Are you sure you haven't forgotten anything?' mother asked, looking down from the jetty into the loaded *Swallow*. 'It's very seldom people go on a long voyage without forgetting something.'

'We've got everything that was on my list,' said Mate Susan.

'Everything?' said mother.

'Mother, what are you holding behind your back?' asked Titty, and mother held out a packet of a dozen boxes of matches.

'One might almost say, By Gum,' said John. 'We could never have lit the fire without them.'

They said their farewells on the jetty.

'If you are ready, you'd better start,' said mother.

'Now, Mister Mate,' said Captain John.

'All aboard,' cried Mate Susan.

Roger took his place in the bows. Titty sat on the middle thwart. John hooked the yard to the traveller on the mast, and hauled up the little brown sail and made the halyard fast.

Arthur Ransome
Swallows and Amazons

THE weeks of captivity were changing into months and then slipping imperceptibly into the second year. I was tired of being alone, tired of depending totally upon my memory and of books read long ago. Suddenly there was a tap on my door: as I fastened my blindfold the guard came into the room and handed me something. I could feel that it was a book. 'Read slow' he said. 'We not have many books.' I nervously removed the blindfold and discovered that in my hands I held my first book since being taken captive: *Beyond Euphrates* by that veteran traveller Freya Stark.

It was cold and my cell was damp. I wrapped my blanket around my shoulders, made myself as comfortable as possible on the floor and began to read. I was delighted to find a rough and ready map at the front of the book – when one has been confined for months, maps provide yet another way for the prisoner to escape in imagination. Before reading the book I used the map to 'walk' along the shores of the Mediterranean – travel over the mountains to the Caspian Sea and trek to the Persian Gulf.

Later, I discovered something of the strange history of this first book given to me in my cell. When John McCarthy and I were exchanging stories in the final months of our captivity I told him about *Beyond Euphrates*. He looked at me in surprise. 'That', he said, 'was the very book I was carrying when I was captured. My mother gave it to me as a birthday present.' It was the last gift John was to receive from his mother as she died while he was still incarcerated in the Lebanon.

A part of the first chapter gives an indication of this superb book:

The word ecstasy is always related to some sort of discovery, a *novelty* to sense or spirit, and it is in search of this word that, in love, in religion, in art or in travel, the adventurous are ready to face the unknown. As we zigzagged down the Adriatic, with that double current which already the ancients recognized as unpleasant, I roused myself at every shore interval to feel interest and pleasure, in Fiume, Split, Bari and Brindisi: but it was Ithaca in the twilight that first revealed the magic word. We had been soothed by quieter waters in the lee of Cephalonia and were slipping in among islands across the Ionian sea: and I asked a name casually, and – steep and unexpected, with all her legends about her – Ithaca was there on the starboard bow.

Every day after that was enchanted. The gulfs of Patras and Corinth, the light of Athens washed in milk and honey, islands in sapphire seas, Rhodes where history lies sleeping – her streets and walls still surrounded by Turkish cemeteries, turbaned headstones askew among the iris – the first of the East, friendly, dingy, dignified and unknown, in Alexandretta and Antioch; and the drive through the stridency of Beirut into stony valleys, to the ridges of Lebanon . . .

The life I left behind me had given, without my knowing it, some of the necessary ingredients for travel. In the first place, I had learnt to rely on myself; not in matters of ordinary efficiency such as the reading of time-tables (which I have never been able to master) and catching of trains, but in a more subtle way: my mother had lived many years out of England, in a voluntary exile, doubtfully received in Italy, and this existence, separated from all the usual props external to ourselves by which we are supported, gave, I think, a certain directness of judgement both to my sister and to me. Without anything particular in the nature of a 'setting', we had nothing but our own intrinsic selves to rely on, and came to look naturally at the intrinsic qualities of other people. Perhaps this is the most important of all assets a traveller can possess, for it minimizes barriers, whether of nationality, race or caste; and in fact I have never been able to feel that human beings differ except in things far more deeply rooted than their manners, habits or outward appearances or colours.

Another quality, produced at first by my father's rigorous teaching of endurance, and secondly by the financial ups and downs of our youth, was a certain indifference to circumstances. I had realized, by wanting them, how desirable many things are, but had also come to see how much of life can be enjoyed without them; and had learnt and have continued to learn that comfortable things like incomes are the servants and not the masters of our days (especially in a good climate).

Freya Stark
Beyond Euphrates

As a boy I sang in the Church Choir. Sunday by Sunday the language of *The Book of Common Prayer* imprinted itself on my subconscious so that when I found myself totally alone without even a Prayer Book I could recall that which I had learnt effortlessly forty years earlier. Most mornings I would say the Communion Service silently to myself and in the evenings would recite Evening Prayer. Sometimes this made me feel a little better: most of the time I was hardly aware of any difference. The prayers, however, helped me to find a structure in my solitary day and helped me to look outside myself towards God. I was learning how unwise it is to depend too much upon feelings.

I rarely used extempore prayer as I felt this could lead me into pleading with God. I did not want to do that if I could help it. I believe that prayer should be expressive of a relationship rather than the constant repetition of a series of demands.

Each day I started with the General Confession:
it is simple, direct and beautiful.

Almighty and most merciful Father;
We have erred, and strayed from thy ways
    like lost sheep.
We have followed too much the devices and
    desires of our own hearts.
We have offended against thy holy laws.
We have left undone those things which we
    ought to have done.
And we have done those things which we
    ought not to have done;
And there is no health in us.
But thou, O Lord, have mercy upon us,
    miserable offenders.
Spare thou them, O God, which confess their
    faults.
Restore thou them that are penitent;
According to thy promises declared unto
    mankind in Christ Jesu our Lord.
And grant, O most merciful Father, for his
    sake;

That we may hereafter live a godly,
    righteous, and sober life,
To the glory of thy holy Name.
Amen.

The Book of Common Prayer

ALTHOUGH I could not remember very many of the Psalms by heart I was able to bring to mind verses from a number of them. During the days when I had been able to walk freely in Lebanon I often looked towards the mountains which would be covered with snow, while down by the shore it was warm and sunny. Psalm 121 frequently came to mind and I often repeated it facing the only view I had: a damp bare wall.

I will lift up mine eyes unto the hills:
from whence cometh my help.

My help cometh from the Lord:
who hath made heaven and earth.

He will not suffer thy foot to be moved:
he that keepeth thee will not sleep.

Behold, he that keepeth Israel:
shall neither slumber nor sleep.

The Lord himself is thy keeper:
the Lord is thy defence upon thy right hand.

So that the sun shall not burn thee by day:
neither the moon by night.

The Lord shall preserve thee from all evil:
yea, it is even he that shall keep thy soul.
The Lord shall preserve thy going out, and
thy coming in:
from this time forth for evermore.

The Book of Common Prayer

Eventually I received a Prayer Book in most unusual circumstances. Some years earlier when I had been attempting to work for the release of American hostages I visited the Presiding Bishop of the Anglican Church in New York. He signed a small presentation Prayer Book and asked if I would attempt to get it to the hostages when I next visited Beirut. During my next meeting with one of the hostage takers, I handed him the book and asked him if he would give it to the Americans in captivity. He was most suspicious. 'What is this secret message?' he said, pointing to the Bishop's signature. He took hold of the coloured markers – 'Are these secret codes?' I explained, but he was hardly satisfied, although he took the book without further comment. Years later, among the books delivered to my cell was the very same Prayer Book. The spine was broken, the signed page had been torn out and the markers were gone: otherwise the book was intact. As I picked it up, I noticed a small piece of paper inserted at a page indicating prayers to be said in time of sickness. I shall probably never know who used that Prayer Book: it stayed with me for many months until one day a guard took it away and I never saw it again.

AFTER reading *Taken on Trust* one or two people expressed surprise that I had not seemed to find greater comfort in prayer. My faith was certainly a help: it enabled me to maintain hope, and the regular structure of daily prayer helped me to keep going. But I have never believed that prayer brings false comfort and there are occasions when it seems that one is left comfortless. All human beings suffer and thousands have suffered far more than I. Faith does not insulate us from suffering but it certainly makes it possible for us to move through the experience and in many cases enables something creative to emerge.

As a boy of thirteen I was given a book about prayer, which I found totally unreadable. It was entitled *In the Secret Place Most High* and the secrets of that place remain a mystery to me as, over forty years later, I have still to read all of it! That book put me off reading about prayer for years. When I was a student and had to read about the subject I came across a book, *The Venture of Prayer*, which was to make a deep impression upon me. It was written by Hubert Northcott. Father Northcott belonged to the Anglican Community of the Resurrection in Mirfield, Yorkshire. After reading his book, I travelled to Mirfield to meet and discuss with him. He was then an elderly man, wise and patient.

Following my meeting with Hubert Northcott I took an important and difficult step along the road towards deeper self-knowledge and made my first oral confession. I was quite terrified at the prospect of revealing my most private failings before another but took courage and did so. It was a small but important step in my life. One of the reasons this step had significance was that I began to learn what a great capacity I, in company with most human beings, have for self-deception. Objective comments, be they from confessor, therapist or friend seem to me to be vital if one would grow up. They are rarely easy to accept.

In any human family each child has its own peculiar approach to its father or mother; no one is quite like the others. The wise parent recognizes this and deals with each accordingly. If the undemonstrative child tries to imitate the ebullient affection of its sister, it at once becomes unreal and spoils, instead of deepening, its communion with its father. It is something like that with God and ourselves. Each of us has his own way of approach – an intimate personal matter. There is no formula of devotion to take its place. We may get enormous help from the writings of the great masters on the spiritual life. They can aid us in learning the ways of prayer, and sometimes some method suggested by them seems exactly to meet our need for the moment. But sooner or later, as a method, it fails us, and we are left once more face to face with God, helpless 'and with no language but a cry'. We may have learnt much in the meantime, but now we have to assimilate what we have learnt, apparently by losing it all, so that God may have His own way with us and that the personal relationship goes on deepening. And the deeper it gets the more method-less it becomes, as the Flemish mystic, Ruysbroeck, has so beautifully and forcibly described. This is why all attempts at classifying the mystical states of prayer are so unsatisfactory, and why writers differ so much amongst themselves in their attempts to do so. Just as one seems to have found the key, the experience of others breaks through his classifications. St Teresa draws the line sharply between 'mystical theology' and other types of prayer: St John of the Cross is much less definite: he would admit the presence of infused contemplation, i.e. St Teresa's 'mystical theology', further down the scale. Both of these classic writers regard 'spiritual marriage' as the goal of prayer. St Marie de l'Incarnation (the 'St Teresa of Canada', as she has been called) seems to experience stages beyond that.

Hubert Northcott CR
The Venture of Prayer

NEGOTIATING for the release of hostages is often a tedious business. One has to spend long periods of time alone waiting for a telephone call or for a message to come over the radio. At such times it is difficult to concentrate because the tensions of the situation are considerable. I always took books with me as a means of coping with such situations and the book I had when I was taken into captivity was *The Mathematical Experience* by Philip Davis and Reuben Hersh. I have never been any good whatsoever at mathematics but my interest in the subject was stimulated when, in my late teens, I began to read of the relationship between mathematics and philosophy. If only my first maths teachers had had a little more imagination I might have been captivated by the subject at school.

While in captivity, and before receiving any books, I spent a great deal of time doing mental arithmetic. Not only was it a way of keeping my mind active but also as a means of striving for inner harmony when there was a real possibility of disintegration.

Mathematics may be regarded as a creative art, and one who certainly believed this to be so was the mathematician G.H. Hardy. Lionel Elvin, Emeritus Professor of Education (London), once told me a story concerning Hardy. On the morning of the publication of Hardy's *A Mathematician's Apology*, Elvin was walking along Trinity Street in Cambridge. He saw the book, bought it and returned to his room to read. Later in the morning he went to Matthew's Café, now long gone, and spotted Hardy, whom he had not previously met. Elvin went over and said, 'I've already read your book.' 'Oh,' said Hardy, 'How did you get on with it?' 'Well,' replied Elvin, 'you gave two examples. I could do one but not the other.' Hardy bade the young man sit down and with the aid of several table napkins demonstrated his second proof. As Hardy was considered to be a rather shy, man, Lionel Elvin had done rather well.

One does not need to be a mathematician, nor indeed a scholar, to enjoy Hardy's writing.

I propose to put forward an apology for mathematics; and I may be told that it needs none, since there are now few studies more generally recognized, for good reasons or bad, as profitable and praiseworthy. This may be true; indeed it is probable, since the sensational triumphs of Einstein, that stellar astronomy and atomic physics are the only sciences which stand higher in popular estimation. A mathematician need not now consider himself on the defensive. He does not have to meet the sort of opposition described by Bradley in the admirable defence of metaphysics which forms the introduction to *Appearance and Reality*.

A metaphysician, says Bradley, will be told that 'metaphysical knowledge is wholly impossible', or that 'even if possible to a certain degree, it is practically no knowledge worth the name'. 'The same problems,' he will hear, 'the same disputes, the same sheer failure. Why not abandon it and come out? Is there nothing else more worth your labour?' There is no one so stupid as to use this sort of language about mathematics. The mass of mathematical truth is obvious and imposing; its practical applications, the bridges and steam-engines and dynamos, obtrude themselves on the dullest imagination. The public does not need to be convinced that there is something in mathematics.

All this is in its way very comforting to mathematicians, but it is hardly possible for a genuine mathematician to be content with it. Any genuine mathematician must feel that it is not on these crude achievements that the real case for mathematics rests, that the popular reputation of mathematics is based largely on ignorance and confusion, and that there is room for a more rational defence. At any rate, I am disposed to try to make one. It should be a simpler task than Bradley's difficult apology.

I shall ask, then, why is it really worth while to make a serious study of mathematics? What is the proper justification of a mathematician's life? And my answers will be, for the most part, such as are to be expected from a mathematician: I think that it is worth while, that there is ample justification. But I should say at once that my defence of mathematics will be a defence of myself, and that my apology is bound to be to some extent egotistical. I should not think it worth while to apologize for my subject if I regarded myself as one of its failures.

Some egotism of this sort is inevitable, and I do not feel that it really needs justi-fication. Good work is not done by 'humble' men. It is one of the first duties of a professor, for example, in any subject, to exaggerate a little both the importance of his subject and his own importance in it. A man who is always asking 'Is what I do worth while?' and 'Am I the right person to do it?'

will always be ineffective himself and a discouragement to others. He must shut his eyes a little and think a little more of his subject and himself than they deserve. This is not too difficult: it is harder not to make his subject and himself ridiculous by shutting his eyes too tightly.

G.H. Hardy
A Mathematician's Apology

ISOLATION encourages introspection and one had to beware of becoming morose. Apart from losing myself in calculations, I spent hours composing comic verse. My compositions were so long and so complicated that they are now, mercifully, quite beyond recall.

One marvellous 'poet' who took himself very seriously was the immortal William McGonagall. His collected verse, doggerel – call it what you will – often came to mind and caused me to smile. I have never committed his work to memory but he has a place in my affections. Here is an example:

ADDRESS TO SHAKESPEARE

Immortal! William Shakespeare, there's none
     you can excel,
You have drawn out your characters
     remarkably well,
Which is a delight to see enacted upon the
     stage –

For instance, the love-sick Romeo, or
    Othello, in a rage;
His writings are a treasure, which the world
    cannot repay,
He was the greatest poet of the past or of the
    present day –
Also the greatest dramatist, and is worthy of
    the name,
I'm afraid that the world shall never look
    upon his like again.
His tragedy of Hamlet is moral and
    sublime,
And for purity of language, nothing can be
    more fine –
For instance, to hear the fair Ophelia making
    her moan,
At her father's grave, sad and alone . . .
In his beautiful play, *As You Like It*, one
    passage is very fine,
Just for instance in the forest of Arden, the
    language is sublime,
Where Orlando speaks of his Rosalind, most
    lovely and divine,

And no other poet I am sure has written
    anything more fine;
His language is spoken in the Church and by
    the Advocate at the bar,
Here and there and everywhere throughout
    the world afar;
His writings abound with gospel truthes,
    moral and sublime,
And I'm sure in my opinion they are
    surpassing fine;
In his beautiful tragedy of Othello, one
    passage is very fine,
Just for instance where Cassio looses his
    lieutenancy
    . . . By drinking too much wine;
And in grief he exclaims, 'Oh! that men
    should put an
Enemy in their mouths to steal away their
    brains.'
In his great tragedy of Richard the III, one
    passage is very fine
Where the Duchess of York invokes the aid
    of the Divine

For to protect her innocent babes from the
    murderer's uplifted hand,
And smite him powerless, and save her
    babes, I'm sure 'tis really grand.
Immortal! Bard of Avon, your writings are
    divine,
And will live in the memories of your
    admirers until the end of time;
Your plays are read in family circles with
    wonder and delight,
While seated around the fireside on a cold
    winter's night.

The Complete McGonagall

My memory for rhymes and poetry was limited, and my mind went back across the years in an attempt to recover the residue of works long buried in memory. I struggled to bring to mind parts of Byron's *The Prisoner of Chillon* but could only remember occasional lines. As my black beard gradually turned white I remembered the first line of the sonnet: *My hair is grey, but not with years . . .*

On my release, this particular work was drawn to my attention in an unusual way. On leaving the RAF base at Lyneham in Wiltshire after my return to England, I went with my family to the West Indies for a holiday. We stayed in a house by the sea and enjoyed our first experience of being together for years. To our surprise we discovered that a near neighbour, also on holiday, was the former Prime Minister, Margaret Thatcher. Frances and I were invited to spend an evening with her family. Before we left, Mrs Thatcher astounded us by reciting from memory a long passage from *The Prisoner of Chillon*.

In this collection it is possible only to include a short extract and I have chosen stanzas XI and XII. The final lines of stanza XII remind me of a particular event in captivity. Each day I was allowed a few minutes in the bathroom; one day when I was taking a shower I managed to look through a tiny window which the guard had left open by mistake. At that time I was being kept on the fourth or fifth floor of an apartment block and in the street below I could see a lady carrying a bunch of flowers. They looked so colourful that the memory stayed with me throughout the day.

XI

A kind of change came to my fate,
My keepers grew compassionate;
I know not what had made them so,
They were inured to sights of woe
But so it was:-my broken chain
With links unfastened did remain,
And it was liberty to stride
Along my cell from side to side,

And up and down, and then athwart,
And tread it over every part;
And round the pillars one by one,
Returning where my walk begun,
Avoiding only, as I trod,
My brothers' graves without a sod;
For if I thought with heedless tread
My step profaned their lowly bed,
My breath came gaspingly and thick,
And my crush'd heart felt blind and
    sick.

XII

I made a footing in the wall,
It was not therefrom to escape,
For I had buried one and all
Who loved me in a human shape;
And the whole earth would henceforth be
A wider prison unto me:
No child, no sire, no kin had I,
No partner in my misery;
I thought of this and I was glad,
For thought of them had made me mad;

But I was curious to ascend
To my barr'd windows and to bend
Once more, upon the mountains high,
The quiet of a loving eye.

Lord Byron
The Prisoner of Chillon

ANOTHER way of passing the time without books was to make imaginary journeys. Sometimes I would pack my belongings and set out on a long journey by train. I would attempt to time the journey and would conjure up the different views from the window of the carriage.

The eminent historian A.L. Rowse is also a poet and I like his work very much. He reminds me of John Betjeman. I have included his poem 'In the Train to Cambridge'.

Canals, bridges, back gardens,
Monday and the washing hanging out on
    lines,
the black and white map of the cows,
the grey stubble golden in the morning light:
the train chugs on through the English fields,
a black colt, ears pricked forward,
alert, enquiring at an unfamiliar noise,
the combed and harrowed fields,
moving shadows, the bright sun
upon hands, the open pages of a book:

Marsh Gibbon and people asleep in the
    compartment,
the plume of smoke moving across green
    slopes,
four plovers rise from a furrow into flight,
a spire pricks the horizon: Steeple Claydon,
a country lane leads into the beckoning distance
and we move on through pastoral
    Buckinghamshire:
Swanbourne and a touzled wood of oaks,
rooks foraging among the furrows,
sun-glitter on water, the February heat-haze,
catkins bursting, pear-blossom, blackthorn,
    prunus in flower,
the serrated ridge of pine-woods:
a lyric thrush calls the little place alive
where the train stops, nameless, unknown:
Gamlingay and the music of a tractor in the
    afternoon,
a yew tree nods its seeding plumes over a
    country platform,
a horse ploughing in the distance the rich
    black earth

(Is my team ploughing, that I was used to
    drive
And hear the harness jingle when I was man
    alive?)
So passes the commerce of the fields,
So passes the cortège of the train,
Bearing these fragile fruits
Of momentary happiness.

A.L. Rowse
'In the Train to Cambridge'

MONTHS had passed since I received Freya Stark's *Beyond Euphrates*. Although I asked almost daily for another book nothing was given to me and I was forced to continue to search my memory and use my imagination. Then, one day, quite out of the blue, the guard handed me a book. He repeated a phase which was to become only too familiar – 'Read slow'.

The book was an American school textbook detailing the history of slavery in the USA. I read it slowly three or four times until I could remember whole passages by heart. It had a salutory effect. When I felt like complaining about being chained day and night I had only to remember whole generations of slaves who spent their lives in chains. This made my own situation a little more bearable.

While I have been compiling this collection I have also been reading the books submitted for the 1995 Whitbread prize. One of them, *The Longest Memory* by the Guyanan writer, Fred D'Aguiar, is a moving novel of life on a Virginia plantation in 1810. In powerful direct prose, the author describes profound suffering. Here a slave speaks of the pain of remembering: all prisoners know something of that kind of pain . . .

The future is just more of the past waiting to happen. You do not want to know my past nor do you want to know my name for the simple reason that I have none and would have to make it up to please you. What my eyes say has never been true. All these years of my life are in my hands, not in these eyes or even in this head. I woke up one day before the estate stirred, tiptoed over my workmates, former playmates and bedfellows and everything else to do with robbed intimacy, unlatched the door, confronted a damp, starlit morning and decided that from this day I had no name. I was just boy, mule, nigger, slave or whatever else anyone chose to call me. I have been called many other things besides. My eyes are bloodshot and rheumy. I have not been crying: I don't do that anymore. The last time I cried was over the pointless death of a boy I loved as my own. I swore it would be the last time because it hurt more than any pain I'd felt before or since. I never knew crying could take over a body so, rock it, shake it, rattle it, thump it so that the body feels wrecked and cries without tears or movement of any kind, out of sheer exhaustion, except for that moan, groan, hoarse, bass wail. That was me over the whipping of a boy who had to know better somehow and would have learned with a good talking to, or even a beating in these circumstances but not this, not this. I don't want to remember. Memory hurts. Like crying. But still and deep. Memory rises to the skin then I can't be touched. I hurt all over, my bones ache, my teeth loosen in their gums, my nose bleeds. Don't make me remember. I forget as hard as I can.

Fred D'Aguiar
The Longest Memory

67

MY daily routine changed rarely. Sleeping on the floor had ceased to worry me. Prayers from the mosque woke me at daybreak. If I was fortunate I could turn over and return to the security of sleep. It could be anything from two to five hours until the guard entered with breakfast: bread, lebne (rather like yoghurt) and a cup of tea. An hour later my chain was unlocked and I was allowed to visit the bathroom for five minutes or so. Then I was returned to my cell, the chain locked and the day stretched before me like a mighty ocean. I tried not to allow my mind to drift into despair. First, I would say my prayers and then, select a topic to think, or dream about. Some days I would write my autobiography in my head. At others I would choose to dream. Often I would imagine that I was about to sail around the world. I would provision my boat with everything I considered necessary then set sail.

Gavin Young sailed around the world and wrote about his experience in *Slow Boat*

Home. I have to agree with him when he writes about Ascension Island as 'an odd and unappealing place'. My wife and I thought exactly the same when we visited the Island briefly en route for the Falklands in 1992, although we did meet some most hospitable residents. On our return journey, we landed on Ascension in the middle of the night. We were quickly driven to the golf course where one of our party fulfilled a lifelong ambition by driving off from the first tee! It is reputed to be one of the most remote and difficult courses in the world. Perhaps our golfing friend had read the following passage . . .

> *This much is certain, men and women*
> *walking alone on the island amidst the*
> *volcanic clinkers, are liable to take*
> *sudden panic, running this way or that,*
> *or collapsing to the ground and*
> *remaining motionless with terror. Some*
> *have been known to disappear. This is*
> *why the British community arrange*
> *some social function or sporting event*

*for every day of the week to keep them
from brooding about the mysterious
atmosphere.**

The Cable and Wireless people on the island
laugh at this, but Alan Nicholson, a communications expert, rattled off a list of
recent ghostly apparitions he had heard of
from apparently level-headed people – a
woman in white, an invisible man who
clambered into bed with almost anyone
who slept in a particular house, an evil-
faced marine in a nineteenth-century red
uniform coat, and more . . .

The *Pep Sirius* would only be a day or two
in Ascension – the chief engineer had
broken his leg falling on deck and the
island's doctor was making sure it was well
plastered. The island was an air base, an
essential refuelling stop conveniently situated between Britain and the Falkland
Islands. All visitors to the Falklands had

* From a Scottish magazine, the *Bulletin*, 1936.

perforce to fly via Ascension; Thatcher herself had done so. But fortunately for me, since I find air bases as boring as factories, most of that technical activity was tucked away on another side of the island.

It is an odd and unappealing place. Unlike Robinson Crusoe and St Helena, it has a dead feeling. The boobies, wideawake terns, noddies, canaries and waxbills are its only natural inhabitants, somehow surviving the roar of military aircraft over their nesting grounds. But there are no indigenous humans, just British and American servicemen and communications experts, a few Saints to serve them, and a large number of graves and ghosts. I took away a souvenir lump of shiny black obsidian that I found in a shallow valley in a volcanic waste where several wild donkeys snuffled among the clinkers looking for God knows what.

I was delighted to come once more upon the tracks of that 'eminent and excellent buccaneer' Captain William Dampier, whom I had last seen, so to speak, on Juan Fernandez in company with Captain Woodes Rogers in 1709, rescuing Alexander Selkirk. Returning from the Far East, Dampier's ship *Roebuck* had been wrecked on Ascension Island in 1701. He and his men scrambled ashore with sufficient stores but no drinking water, a serious predicament on what was little more than a burnt-out volcano. Needless to say, the dauntless Dampier discovered a tree with an anchor carved on it and a date, 1642, near which a tiny spring gave forth a drip of water but enough to wash down the land crabs, boobies and goats that were their basic diet. I trudged up to the spring, known to this day as Dampier's Drip, and paid my respects to the old seadog once again.

Gavin Young
Slow Boat Home

THE book on slavery in the USA, which had been with me for several weeks, was finally taken away. I imagined that it was given to another prisoner although I was never told. Eventually another paperback was put into my hands. 'This very good book. You read' said my guard earnestly. When he left the room I eagerly examined the volume: it was an English rendering of the Koran. I started to read the introductory notes written by the translator, an Arabist from Cambridge. He concluded his remarks by saying that the book had brought him much comfort during a time when he was suffering acute personal distress. This human comment tucked away in the middle of an academic note moved me deeply. I wondered what had caused the poor man so much suffering and I also wondered if The Koran would bring me similar consolation.

In the past I had dipped into it and now I read it from cover to cover but I regret to say that it did not help me very much. I had been told that to appreciate the Koran one needed to know Arabic. As the guards would not, under any circumstances, allow me to learn that language I had to be content with the English version. It is also very possible that, as I was suffering at the hands of those who claimed to follow its precepts, I was not in the best frame of mind to find inspiration from the Koran. An apologist, the Revd G. Margoliouth has written an introduction to Rodwell's translation and, although this book is somewhat dated, he does explain why I in company with many other Westerners might find the Koran difficult.

The style in which the Koran is written requires some special attention in this introduction. The literary form is for the most part different from anything else we know. In its finest passages we indeed seem to hear a voice akin to that of the ancient Hebrew prophets, but there is much in the book which Europeans usually regard as faulty. The tendency to repetition which is an inherent characteristic of the Semitic mind appears here in an exaggerated form, and there is in addition much in the Koran which strikes us as wild and fantastic. The most unfavourable criticism ever passed on Muhammed's style has in fact been penned by the prophet's greatest British admirer, Carlyle himself; and there are probably many now who find themselves in the same dilemma with that great writer.

The fault appears, however, to lie partly in our difficulty to appreciate the psychology of the Arab prophet. We must, in order to do him justice, give full consideration to his temperament and to the condition of things around him. We are here in touch with an untutored but fervent mind, trying to realise itself and to assimilate certain great truths which have been powerfully borne in upon him, in order to impart them in a convincing form to his fellow-tribesmen. He is surrounded by obstacles of every kind, yet he manfully struggles on with the message that is within him. Learning he has none, or next to none. His chief objects of knowledge are floating stories and traditions largely picked up from hearsay, and his over-wrought mind is his only teacher. The literary compositions to which he had ever listened were the half-cultured, yet often wildly powerful rhapsodies of early Arabian minstrels, akin to Ossian rather than to anything else within our knowledge. What wonder then that his Koran took a form which to our colder temperaments sounds strange, unbalanced, and fantastic?

G. Margoliouth
Introduction to J.M. Rodwell's
translation of *The Koran*

I would like this book to have within it a small passage from an English rendering of the Koran and so I am including some lines which will be very familiar to Muslims and known also to many non-Muslims.

He is God, there is no God but He.
He is the Knower of the unseen and the
    visible;
He is the all-merciful, the all-Compassionate.

He is God, there is no God but He.
He is the King, the Holy, the Peaceable,
The Faithful, the Preserver.
The Mighty; the Compeller, the Sublime.
Glory be to God, above that they associate!

He is God, the Creator, the Maker, the Shaper.
To Him belong the Names Most Beautiful.
All that is in the heavens and earth
    magnifies Him;
He is the Mighty, the Wise.

The Koran 59.22–4.

As each day passed it seemed to me increasingly likely that I was in for a long stay. Already more than a year had gone by and there was no sign of release. I did not know how to prepare myself for an even longer period of solitary imprisonment. In the days when I was allowed off the chain for an hour or so I would walk in order to keep my body as fit as possible but even that was now denied me. I knew that it was vital to keep my mind alive and to continue to exercise memory in order to keep my brain working. I tried to remember the books I had read which detailed experiences in prison. One of the most moving, but hardly comforting, was *Darkness at Noon* by Arthur Koestler. Shortly before my own detention I had presented the Koestler awards in London. These are made annually to inmates of British prisons who have produced a painting or other work of art.

Any prisoner who reads *Darkness at Noon* will recognise that the author is speaking directly from his own experience.

Rubashov leant his forehead against the window and looked down into the yard. He was tired in the legs and dizzy in the head from walking up and down. He looked at his watch; a quarter to twelve; he had been walking to and fro in his cell for nearly four hours on end, since first the *Pietà* had occurred to him. It did not surprise him; he was well enough acquainted with the day-dreams of imprisonment, with the intoxication which emanates from the whitewashed walls. He remembered a younger comrade, by profession a hairdresser's assistant, telling him how, in his second and worst year of solitary confinement, he had dreamed for seven hours on end with his eyes open; in doing so he had walked twenty-eight kilometres, in a cell five paces long, and had blistered his feet without noticing it.

This time, however, it had come rather quickly; already, the first day, the vice had befallen him, whereas during his previous experiences it had started only after several weeks. Another strange thing was that he had thought of the past; chronic prison day-dreamers dreamed nearly always of the future – and of the past only as it might have been, never as it actually *had* been. Rubashov wondered what other surprises his mental apparatus held in store for him. He knew from experience that confrontation with death always altered the mechanism of thought and caused the most surprising reactions – like the movements of a compass brought close to the magnetic pole.

The sky was still heavy with an imminent fall of snow; in the courtyard two men were doing their daily walk on the shovelled path. One of the two repeatedly looked up at Rubashov's window – apparently the news of his arrest had already spread. He was an emaciated man with a yellow skin and a hare-lip, wearing a thin waterproof which he clutched round his shoulders as if freezing. The other man was older and had wrapped a blanket round himself. They did not speak to each other during their round, and after ten minutes they were fetched back into the building by an official in uniform with a rubber truncheon and a revolver. The door in which the official waited for them lay exactly opposite Rubashov's window; before it closed behind the man with the hare-lip, he once more looked up towards Rubashov. He certainly could not see Rubashov, whose window must have appeared quite dark from the courtyard; yet his eyes lingered on the window searchingly. I see you and do not know you; you cannot see me and yet obviously you know me, thought Rubashov. He sat down on the bed and tapped to No. 402:

WHO ARE THEY?

He thought that No. 402 was probably offended and would not answer. But the officer did not seem to bear grudges; he answered immediately:

POLITICAL.

Rubashov was surprised; he had held the thin man with the hare-lip for a criminal.

OF YOUR SORT? he asked.

NO – OF YOURS, tapped No. 402, in all probability grinning with a certain satisfaction. The next sentence was louder – tapped with the monocle, perhaps.

HARE-LIP, MY NEIGHBOUR, NO. 400, WAS TORTURED YESTERDAY.

Rubashov remained silent a minute and rubbed his pince-nez on his sleeve, although he was only using it to tap with. He first wanted to ask 'Why?' but tapped instead:

HOW?

402 tapped back drily:

STEAMBATH.

Rubashov had been beaten up repeatedly during his last imprisonment, but of this method he only knew by hearsay. He had learned that every *known* physical pain was bearable; if one knew beforehand exactly what was going to happen to one, one stood it as a surgical operation – for instance, the extraction of a tooth. Really bad was only the unknown, which gave one no chance to

foresee one's reactions and no scale to calculate one's capacity of resistance. And the
worst was the fear that one would then do or
say something which could not be recalled.

WHY? asked Rubashov.

POLITICAL DIVERGENCIES, tapped No.
402 ironically.

Rubashov put his pince-nez on again and
felt in his pocket for his cigarette case. He
had only two cigarettes left. Then he tapped:

AND HOW ARE THINGS WITH YOU?

THANKS, VERY WELL . . . tapped No.
402 and dropped the conversation.

Rubashov shrugged his shoulders; he lit his
last cigarette but one and resumed his walking
up and down. Strangely enough, what was in
store for him made him nearly glad. He felt his
stale melancholia leave him, his head become
clearer, his nerves tauten. He washed face,
arms and chest in cold water over the wash-
basin, rinsed his mouth and dried himself with
his handkerchief. He whistled a few bars and
smiled – he was always hopelessly out of tune,

and only a few days ago somebody had said to him: 'If No. 1 were musical, he would long ago have found a pretext to have you shot.'

'He will anyhow,' he had answered, without seriously believing it.

He lit his last cigarette and with a clear head began to work out the line to take when he would be brought up for cross-examination. He was filled by the same quiet and serene self-confidence as he had felt as a student before a particularly difficult examination. He called to memory every particular he knew about the subject 'steambath'. He imagined the situation in detail and tried to analyse the physical sensations to be expected, in order to rid them of their uncanniness. The important thing was not to let oneself be caught unprepared. He now knew for certain that they would not succeed in doing so, any more than had the others over there; he knew he would not say anything he did not want to say. He only wished they would start soon.

His dream came to his mind: Richard and the old taxi-driver pursuing him, because they felt themselves cheated and betrayed by him.

I will pay my fare, he thought with an awkward smile.

His last cigarette was nearly at an end; it was burning his finger-tips; he let it drop. He was about to stamp it out, but thought better of it; he bent down, picked it up and stubbed out the glowing stump slowly on the back of his hand, between the blue snaky veins. He drew out this procedure for exactly half a minute, checking it by the seconds hand of his watch. He was pleased with himself: his hand had not twitched once during the thirty seconds. Then he continued his walk.

The eye which had been observing him for several minutes through the spy-hole withdrew.

Arthur Koestler
Darkness at Noon

ANOTHER way of escaping from the crushing boredom of captivity was to take long walks in my imagination. Throughout my life I have enjoyed walking through cities. London, Bombay, Shanghai, New York, Melbourne: I have walked them all. My method has been to set out with a guide book and let the city unfold. Conducted tours have never appealed to me.

My reactions to New York have always been mixed. On the one hand the crime and squalor can be utterly depressing: on the other, I love the verve and dynamism of the city. It is exhilarating to walk alongside Central Park on a cold crisp Sunday morning when the sky is a clear bright blue and the traffic is light.

Following my release, I returned to New York to visit old friends. It was more than five years since I had last been in the city and I decided that I would follow my customary practice and visit the Tall Man's shop to buy one or two things.

When I arrived at the location there was no sign of the building. A police car stopped and the driver leaned out of the window. 'Hi Terry,' he shouted. 'Are you lost?' I explained what I was looking for. He smiled. 'They moved years ago. Jump in the back – we'll take you.'

Eric Newby who, incidentally, was a prisoner of war, has written about New York in his book, *A Traveller's Life*.

In the autumn of 1965 I went to New York. This, apart from the pleasurable but abortive visit to *Holiday Magazine* two years previously, was my first visit to the city, and my aim now in going there was to attempt to find out how the impoverished British could survive in it, faced with a strong dollar, and armed with nothing but their native wit and intelligence and a handful of old-fangled pounds.

Starting at the top and working my way downwards through the innumerable strata which make up New York – and which are encountered long before you get down to the mud, sand and gravel, decomposed rock, schist, Inwood limestone and Fordham gneiss on which man-made New York is set up – took a long time, because everything was so different from anything I had known back home in Wimbledon, SW19. Even my favourite author, the American Richard Bissell, on whom up to now I had relied implicitly for information on the New York scene and how to comport oneself within it, was sometimes floored for an answer. The following passage from his book *Say Darling*, which describes how he came to write a musical called *The Pajama Game*, demonstrates this, as well as indicating that it was the sort of problem New Yorkers were having to face up to every day:

In boarding a bus or any public conveyance should the gentleman assist his companion on first, or should he get on first? Suppose I and Miss Gloria Vanderbilt was boarding a bus to go

have a Giant Idaho Potato at
Toffenetti's and I fouled up the
embarkation rites. She would tell
Sinatra I was as square as a coffee table.

So that I would run out of steam before I ran
out of money (I really was playing the game
of doing the whole thing with a minimum of
cash), and eschewing the bus and subway
services for reasons that are immediately
apparent to anyone who has ever been
confronted by them, I carried out my in-
vestigations either on foot or by bike,
starting on Fifth, Park and Madison Ave-
nues. At that time you could still see, not
locked away in huge automobiles but walking the streets of the city, something rare in
Europe – where the waxy, exhumed, dan-
druffy look had spread like the Black Death
– rich, beautiful girls dressed in garments by
Norell, Chanel and Balenciaga bought from
Bergdorf Goodman and Henri Bendel and
similar emporia. In London, where the

daughters of the rich were busy camouflaging themselves as members of the proletariat and taking elocution lessons in Birkenhead, they would have been the daughters of South American ambassadors. Here they were home-grown and could be seen not only in the streets but also up at the Plaza Hotel on Central Park – as I zoomed through the Palm Court around four p.m., too fast for the maître d'hôtel to sit me down to a muffin – taking tea with their mothers, some of whom were wearing the most fantastic hats. (One of the treats I was preparing for the penniless readers of my column was a free zoom through the Plaza.)

Eric Newby
A Traveller's Life

WHILE visiting New York I would often stay with friends in Brooklyn which is as culturally varied today as it was when Betty Smith was growing up there during the early part of the twentieth century.

I first came across her classic novel *A Tree Grows in Brooklyn* when a tattered copy was given to me by my guard. Drawing on personal experiences the author describes family life in Brooklyn as she remembered it.

Although the Nolans of Brooklyn are aware of their Irish roots, Francie is proud to be an American. The warmth and humour of the lovely book revived many memories and cheered several dull days.

Francie was the only one in her classroom whose parents were American-born. At the beginning of the term, Teacher called the roll and asked each child her lineage. The answers were typical.

'I'm Polish-American. My father was

born in Warsaw.'

'Irish-American. Me fayther and mither were born in County Cork.'

When Nolan was called, Francie answered proudly: 'I'm an American.'

'I *know* you're American,' said the easily exasperated teacher. 'But what's your nationality?'

'American!' insisted Francie even more proudly.

'Will you tell me what your parents are or do I have to send you to the principal?'

'My parents are American. They were born in Brooklyn.'

All the children turned around to look at a little girl whose parents had *not* come from the old country. And when Teacher said: 'Brooklyn? Hm. I guess that makes you American, all right,' Francie was proud and happy. How wonderful was Brooklyn, she thought, when just being born there automatically made you an American!

Papa had told her about this strange neighbourhood: how its families had been Americans for more than a hundred years back: how they were mostly Scotch, English and Welsh extraction. The men worked as cabinet-makers and fine carpenters. They worked with metals: gold, silver and copper.

He promised to take Francie to the Spanish section of Brooklyn some day. There the men worked as cigar-makers, and each chipped in a few pennies a day to hire a man to read to them while they worked. And the man read fine literature.

They walked along the quiet Sunday street. Francie saw a leaf flutter from a tree and she skipped ahead to get it. It was a clear scarlet with an edging of gold. She stared at it, wondering if she'd ever see anything as beautiful again. A woman came from around the corner. She was rouged heavily and wore a feather boa. She smiled at Johnny and said:

'Lonesome, Mister?'

Johnny looked at her a moment before he answered gently:

'No, Sister.'

'Sure?' she inquired archly.

'Sure,' he answered quietly.

She went her way. Francie skipped back and took papa's hand.

'Was that a bad lady, Papa?' she asked eagerly.

'No.'

'But she *looked* bad.'

'There are very few bad people. There are just a lot of people that are unlucky.'

'But she was all painted and . . . '

'She was one who had seen better days.' He liked the phrase. 'Yes, she may have seen better days.' He fell into a thoughtful mood. Francie kept skipping ahead and collecting leaves.

They came upon the school and Francie proudly showed it to papa. The late after-noon sun warmed its softly-coloured bricks and the small-paned windows seemed to dance in the sunshine. Johnny looked at it a long time, then he said:

'Yes, this is the school. This is it.'

Then, as whenever he was moved or stirred, he had to put it into a song. He held his worn derby over his heart, stood up straight looking up at the school house and sang:

> School days, school days,
> Dear old golden rule days,
> Readin' 'n writin' 'n 'rithmetic . . .

To a passing stranger it might have looked silly – Johnny standing there in his greenish tuxedo and fresh linen holding the hand of a thin, ragged child and singing the banal song so un-self-consciously on the street. But to Francie it seemed right and beautiful.

Betty Smith
A Tree Grows in Brooklyn

SHORTLY before my final visit to Beirut and subsequent imprisonment, I visited San Francisco with Frances and our son, Mark. One cold foggy morning we took the ferry across the bay to the Island of Alcatraz. The name is derived from the Spanish word for 'pelican' since the birds were much in evidence when the island was discovered by a Spanish lieutenant in 1775.

Our guide showed us around the once notorious prison, which had been abandoned by the Federal Government in 1963. We were invited to spend a few minutes in what had been a punishment cell and were left in total darkness. The guide told us that some of the most difficult prisoners had been obliged to spend up to seven days in such a place. I shuddered and doubted whether I should be able to last for twenty-four hours.

Alistair Cooke has written a gripping account of his visit to Alcatraz while it was still in use as a prison. I was to remember this during my long years in my own cell in Beirut.

Alcatraz is a 'corrective' prison for men who know how to organize sit-down strikes in state prisons; for incorrigibles; for bred-in-the-bone mischief makers of the Republic; for the men who employ a life sentence as a lifelong challenge to discover, how, with a twisted hairpin or a stolen razor blade, to break away from any prison they are put in.

A removal to Alcatraz is thus considered in the underworld as a kind of general's baton, the reward of distinguished field service that cannot be overlooked. And the guides on the steamers that ply through the riptides close to the island never fail to call off the roster of the incurable desperadoes who have battled the state prisons and landed here: 'Limpy' Cleaver, Machine-Gun Kelly, Gene Colson, and Al Capone. If a man goes through Alcatraz with an impeccable record he may shorten his stretch there; but invariably, on the day of his release, two guards appear from the state prison that could not hold him. A warrant is sworn for his instant arrest, and he goes off in handcuffs back to the state that claims him, for another twenty years, or whatever, or perhaps for life.

I myself seem to have a mystical relation with Alcatraz. On the first day of my honeymoon, in the spring of 1946, I was driving my wife across the four-and-a-half-mile span of the Oakland-Bay Bridge, ticketing the wonders of the bay, and like all newcomers she wanted to see and shudder at Alcatraz. I looked over my steering arm toward the island and saw little puffs of smoke peppering the blue sky. And I said, offhand, 'Down there where the whiffs of grapeshot are coming from.' Well, by the time we got back to the city from a trip to the Berkeley hills, the newspapers were inky with fresh black headlines. The puffs of smoke had not come from a trap-shooting exercise. They announced the now celebrated Battle of Alcatraz. The inmates had seized the arsenal and tied up two guards, whom they subsequently killed. For two days the men shot it out with the guards, and it took the arrival of the Marines to break them.

Again, in 1958, I flew into San Francisco on the last Monday in September and had barely had time to unpack before the wailing of klaxons started, and two men had vanished from Alcatraz.

Now the trick of escaping from Alcatraz by the water route (and unless you have a friend with a silent helicopter there is no other) is worth a little thought, surprisingly more than the men who have tried it have cared to give it. The distance to freedom is, as I said, no more than a mile and a tenth. But it is a ferocious stream that empties into the Pacific with an ebb tide swollen and quickened by the waters of the Sacramento River. Close by the island, even on the most placid days, the water is slashed by riptides and gurgling with whirlpools. You might conceivably plow through these hazards if it were not for the implacable enemy: the extreme, unvarying cold of the water. A guard I met had jumped in one hot afternoon to rescue a mother and child, from one of the staff families, who had been playing by the water's edge and stumbled in. He fished them out in five minutes and was confined to a hospital for two days with chill and shock. The doctors calculate that an average healthy man with a reasonable layer of blubber on his bones could stay alive in these waters for not more than twenty-two minutes. But it takes about forty minutes for a log of wood to achieve the ambition of the inmates, namely to catch the full ebb tide, drift down to the Golden Gate, and be deposited on one of the nearby beaches. In the last twenty-four years, nineteen men have tried it. Five never got beyond the range of the catwalk guns and were shot to death. Twelve were captured in the water, or – feeling the ice around their spleen – chose to slosh back to

the comparative comfort of a longer lifetime on the island. Two vanished and are
presumed long dead.

Mind you, it can be done, but not on the
ebb tide on a foggy night, and not by you or
me, or Al Capone. Johnny Weismuller,
when he was the world's champion swim-
mer, looked the prospect over and thought
better of it. In 1936, Babe Scott, the nine-
teen-year-old daughter of a police sergeant,
made it on the flood tide at high noon, on a
brilliant hot day with an accompanying
launch, nips of brandy, a well-greased
body, a cheering press boat, and several
other amenities which the warden and his
men do not provide for intending escapists.

Alistair Cooke
Talk About America

MANY years ago, while on holiday with my family in Norfolk, we went to spend an afternoon at the small seaside resort of Wells. In the market place there was a man with a large wooden barrow of the kind street traders use. I walked across and examined his stock. The stall was full of 'Everyman' classics and he was selling them off cheaply. I lingered, debating whether or not to make him an offer for all the books. To my everlasting regret, I failed to do so.

The 'Everyman' series was originally published by J.M. Dent, who came as a boy to London to seek his fortune. The verse:

> Everyman. I will go with thee, and be thy guide,
> In thy most need to go by thy side

was printed on the inside front covers of these distinctive volumes.

From my cell I remembered the Everyman books I had collected during my lifetime and thought that it would have been good to have with me the *Meditations* of Marcus Aurelius. This book has been compared to another equally famous work, *The Imitation of Christ* by Thomas à Kempis. Both speak about self-control and that was a quality I needed to understand and practise as best I could.

Marcus Aurelius Antoninus (AD 121–180) was born in the second century of a noble family. Early training in Stoic philosophy taught him to dress plainly, live simply and avoid all softness and luxury. Unlike *The Imitation of Christ*, which was written for others, the *Meditations* are addressed by the writer to himself.

The Tenth Book of the *Meditations* is most eloquent.

Wilt thou one day, my soul, be good, simple, single, naked, plainer to see than the body surrounding thee? Wilt thou one day taste a loving and devoted disposition? Wilt thou one day be filled and without want, craving nothing and desiring nothing, animate or inanimate, for indulgence in pleasures; not time wherein longer to indulge thyself, nor happy situation of place or room or breezes nor harmony of men? Wilt thou rather be satisfied with present circumstance and pleased with all the present, and convince thyself that all is present for thee from the gods and all is well for thee and will be well whatsoever is dear to them to give and whatsoever they purpose to bestow for the sustenance of the perfect living creature, the good and just and beautiful, which begets, sustains, includes and embraces all things that are being resolved into the generation of others like themselves? Wilt thou one day be such as to dwell in the society of gods and men so as neither to find fault at all with them nor to be condemned by them?

Marcus Aurelius
Meditations

At long last the guards managed to get their hands on some more books. Someone would go to a second-hand bookshop, collect several volumes, give them to another person and, after passing through several pairs of hands, the books would eventually arrive at the house in which I was being held. First I received several detective novels which I enjoyed tremendously. This surprised me, because years before I had been put off by the writing of Agatha Christie and thus gave up reading detective stories. One of the first given to me was *Busman's Honeymoon* by Dorothy L Sayers. Her old-fashioned wit made me laugh out loud.

Lord Peter Wimsey is on honeymoon with the former Harriet Vane and has brought his invaluable manservant Bunter. They choose to stay in a remote house in the country and of course become involved in a murder. I enjoyed more than anything the description of the village characters, and I have chosen an extract that introduces the Revd Simon Goodacre, a type of clergyman I have encountered hundreds of times.

The honeymoon couple are having trouble with the chimney. Enter Mr Goodacre, who believes he can solve the problem with a gun!

'I never like the idea of fire-arms,' said Miss Twitterton!

'No, no,' said the vicar. 'Trust me; there will be no ill effects.' He possessed himself of the gun and examined the lock and trigger mechanism with the air of one to whom the theory of ballistics was an open book.

'It's all loaded and ready, sir,' said Mrs Ruddle, proudly conscious of her Bert's efficiency.

Miss Twitterton gave a faint squeak, and the vicar, thoughtfully turning the muzzle of the gun away from her, found himself covering Bunter, who entered at that moment from the passage.

'Excuse me, my lord,' said Bunter, with superb nonchalance but a wary eye; 'there is a person at the door – '

'Just a moment, Bunter,' broke in his master. 'The fireworks are about to begin. The chimney is to be cleared by the natural expansion of gases.'

'Very good, my lord.' Bunter appeared to measure the respective forces of the weapon and the vicar. 'Excuse me, sir. Had you not better permit me – ?'

'No, no,' cried Mr Goodacre. 'Thank you. I can manage it perfectly.' Gun in hand, he plunged head and shoulders beneath the chimney-drape.

'Humph!' said Peter. 'You're a better man than I am, Gunga Din.'

He removed his pipe from his mouth and with his free hand gathered his wife to him. Miss Twitterton, having no husband to cling to, flung herself upon Crutchley for protection, uttering a plaintive cry:

'Oh, Frank! I know I shall scream at the noise.'

'There's no occasion for alarm,' said the vicar, popping out his head like a showman from behind the curtain. 'Now – are we all ready?'

Mr Puffett put on his bowler hat.

'Ruat coelum!' said Peter; and the gun went off.

It exploded like the crack of doom, and it kicked (as Peter had well foreseen) like a carthorse. Gun and gunman rolled together upon the hearth, entangled inextricably in the folds of the drape. As Bunter leaped to the rescue, the loosened soot of centuries came plunging in a mad cascade down the chimney; it met the floor with a soft and deadly violence and mushroomed up in a Stygian cloud, while with it rushed, in a clattering shower, masonry and mortar, jackdaws' nests and the bones of bats and owls, sticks, bricks and metalwork, with fragments of tiles and potsherds. The shrill outcry of Mrs Ruddle and Miss Twitterton was drowned by the eruptive rumble and boom that echoed from bend to bend of the forty-foot flue.

'Oh, rapture!' cried Peter, with his lady in his arms. 'Oh, bountiful Jehovah! Oh, joy for all its former woes a thousand-fold repaid!'

'There!' exclaimed Mr Puffett, triumphantly. 'You can't say as I didn't warn yer.'

Peter opened his mouth to reply, when the sight of Bunter, snorting and blind, and black as any Nubian Venus, struck him speechless with ecstasy.

'Oh, dear!' cried Miss Twitterton. She fluttered round, making helpless little darts at the swaddled shape that was the vicar. 'Oh, dear, dear, dear! Oh, Frank! Oh, goodness!'

'Peter!' panted Harriet.

'I knew it!' said Peter. 'Whoop! I knew it! You blasphemed the aspidistra and something awful *has* come down that chimney!'

'Peter! it's Mr Goodacre in the sheet.'

'Whoop!' said Peter again. He pulled himself together and joined Mr Puffett in unwinding the clerical cocoon; while Mrs Ruddle and Crutchley led away the unfortunate Bunter.

Mr Goodacre emerged in some disorder.

'Not hurt, sir, I hope?' inquired Peter with grave concern.

'Not at all, not at all,' replied the vicar, rubbing his shoulder. 'A little arnica will soon put that to rights!' He smoothed his scanty hair with his hands and fumbled for his glasses. 'I trust the ladies were not unduly alarmed by the explosion. It appears to have been effective.'

'Remarkably so,' said Peter. He pulled a pampas grass from the drain-pipe and poked delicately among the debris, while Harriet, flicking soot from the vicar, was reminded of Alice dusting the White King. 'It's surprising the things you find in old chimneys.'

Dorothy L. Sayers
Busman's Honeymoon

I could fill this book with extracts from crime novels that I enjoyed in Beirut. There is space for only one more. Michael Innes is the pen-name of J.I.M. Stewart of Christ Church, Oxford, who created Inspector John Appleby. To my mind Stewart was a brilliant writer. I am including part of the first chapter of *Appleby's End*, which gives an indication of how much the author can convey in a few words.

I have promised myself that one day, preferably in the winter, I shall go to a small country hotel and take with me a selection of the Innes books I have yet to read. Good food, good walks and good books are my idea of heaven – at least for a few days.

The guard blew his whistle and waved his flag – how weighted with ritual have the railways in their brief century become! – and the train crawled from the little station. The guard walked alongside through the snow-flakes, wistful for that jump-and-swing at an accelerating van that is the very core of the mystery of guarding trains. But the train continued to crawl. Sundry footballers in a glass box, some with legs swung high in air, stood immobile to watch its departure.

The engine tooted. In pinnacled and convoluted automatic machines, memorials of an age wildly prodigal of cast-iron, the slowly moving traveller would have found it possible to remark that the final and unremunerative penny had long since been dropped. Long ago had some fortunate child secured the last brightly wrapped wafer of chocolate; long ago had the last wax vesta released a dubious fragrance from the last cigarette – and the once flamboyant weighing machine, pathetic in its antique inability either to bellow or print, seemed yet, in its forlorn proposal to register a burden of thirty stone, whispering dumbly of dealings with a race of giants before the Flood.

Just such a well-cadenced if vacuous meditation as this might the passenger, drear and bored, have constructed for himself before the guard stepped resignedly aboard, the platform dipped, points sluggishly clanked and the train was in open country once more. Sunday afternoon, which in England subtly spreads itself over the face even of inanimate Nature, stretched to the flat horizon. The fields were clothed in patchy white like half-hearted penitents; here and there cattle stood steamy and dejected, burdened like their fellows in Thomas Hardy's poems with some intuitive low-down on essential despair; and now on the outskirts of a village the train trundled past a yellow brick conventicle constructed on the basis of hardly more cheery theological convictions. Inside the carriage it was cold and beginning to be fuggy as well. The focus of attention was a large glass bowl rather like those used in cemeteries to protect artificial flowers, but here pendulous from the roof and sheltering gas burners of a type judged moderately progressive at the Great Exhibition of 1851. Flanking this were luggage racks of a breadth nicely calculated to cause chronic anxiety in those below. Then came photographs: a beach and promenade densely packed with holiday-makers dressed in heavy mourning: a vast railway hotel standing, Chirico-like, in a mysteriously dispopulated public square: a grove exaggeratedly bosky and vernal, bespattered with tea tables and animated by three stiffly-ranked dryads in the disguise of waitresses.

Under the photographs were the passengers. Over the faces of the passengers, or lying on their knees, or slipped to their feet, were the objects of Sabbath devotion traditional to Englishmen in the lower and middle ranks of society. There were instruments and blunt instruments, packets of weed-killer and bundles of incriminating letters. There were love nests. There were park benches over which white crosses and black circles hung mysteriously in air. There were serious offences and grave charges; there were faces, blurry and odd-angled, of judges, coroners, and detective-inspectors from Scotland Yard. Thin-lipped and driven women stood between policemen outside assize halls; persons now of notorious life lay naked on horse-hair sofas waving rattles, or dangled booted legs over Edwardian tables.

Snow fell outside, as perhaps on half a dozen Sundays in the year. But every Sunday there was this sift and silt of newsprint in the domestic interiors of England. Big money lay in and behind it. In their brief elevation into objects of national curiosity these inconsiderable criminals and furtive amorists were sought out by vast organizations, groomed, glamorized and sub-edited in clifflike buildings, multiplied and distributed with miraculous speed by powerful machines. And thence were sucked into millions of minds. It was the sucking that was really operative in the process: had the suckers not an instinct to suck, it was likely that the vast organizations would find other things to do. And so this laboriously garnered world of crime and misconduct and sensation was, in fact, a mythology – a fleeting and hebdomadal mythology called into being by the obscurely working but infinitely potent creativity of the folk. In the green Arcadian valleys Pan is dead but still a numerous Panisci lurk and follow in the parks. Armies of thieves are still littered under Mercury. The rape of Proserpin – gathering flowers, herself a fairer flower – continues still, and Dis's wagon is a borrowed limousine.

Why in these latter days should the perennial myths have so squalid an embodiment – this same splendid car in which Pluto carried off Demeter's daughter decline into Madame Bovary's patiently perambulating cab? John Appleby, himself a detective-inspector from Scotland Yard and with a weakness for cultivated reverie, had arrived at this large question when the train jerked to a halt. Twisting his neck as he sat cramped in a corner, he peered through the window. Mere dejection seemed to have occasioned this stoppage, and in mere dejection too the countryside was fading on the sight. In a field beyond the telegraph wires there stood a single gaunt tree. A tree, thought Appleby, of infinitely sinister silhouette. But this impression was, of course, a matter of simple projection. From the sog and wash of Sunday newspapers littering the carriage a species of miasma arose and seeped into the mind. And the mind, like a well-fed fire-engine, promptly sprayed this out again upon a waiting and neutral Nature . . .

Appleby stooped and picked up one of the abandoned papers from the floor. It opened on a youngish man, bowler-hatted, well-nourished and – surely – repulsive, standing with a truculently elevated chin before what appeared to be the shell of a burnt-out stable or hovel. Appleby glanced at caption and legend, and sighed. The Gaffer Odgers Murder. Old Gaffer Odgers had been unlovely in life, and in death he had been a faint stench as of roasted carrion. And the bowler-hatted person was Appleby himself. About eight years ago, that had been; and here was somebody writing it up for a new generation of connoisseurs. When current crime fell flat the public was very willing to be regaled from hiding places ten years deep.

Michael Innes
Appleby's End

THE novels, while they lasted, provided an escape, not only from the bleakness of my surroundings but also from the relentless inner examination I was conducting. As I was 'writing' in my head I was also attempting to go more deeply into myself. I tried to examine my motives and to understand more of the complex duality I recognised within. St Paul sums this up in a nutshell: 'For the good that I would I do not: but the evil which I would not, that I do.' (Rom. 7:19) To be really honest about my own human nature was painful.

I had started this journey years ago and had been considerably helped by the writings of C.G. Jung, the Swiss founder of analytical psychology. Jung begins his autobiography with a quote from Coleridge's *Notebooks*:

> He looked at his own Soul
> with a Telescope. What seemed
> all irregular, he saw and
> shewed to be beautiful
> Constellations: and he added

to the Consciousness hidden
worlds within worlds.

I'm afraid that as I examined myself I discovered
that the irregular had hardly been transformed
into that which was beautiful. And yet I wanted
to continue.

Jung speaks about the importance of inner life
in the Prologue to his autobiography, *Memories,
Dreams, Reflections*.

My life is a story of the self-realisation of
the unconscious. Everything in the unconscious seeks outward manifestation, and the
personality too desires to evolve out of its
unconscious conditions and to experience
itself as a whole. I cannot employ the
language of science to trace this process of
growth in myself, for I cannot experience
myself as a scientific problem.

What we are to our inward vision, and
what man appears to be *sub specie aeterni-
tatis*, can only be expressed by way of myth.

Myth is more individual and expresses life more precisely than does science. Science works with concepts of averages which are far too general to do justice to the subjective variety of an individual life.

Thus it is that I have now undertaken, in my eighty-third year, to tell my personal myth. I can only make direct statements, only 'tell stories'. Whether or not the stories are 'true' is not the problem. The only question is whether what I tell is *my* fable, *my* truth.

An autobiography is so difficult to write because we possess no standards, no objective foundation, from which to judge ourselves. There are really no proper bases for comparison. I know that in many things I am not like others, but I do not know what I really am like. Man cannot compare himself with any other creature; he is not a monkey, not a cow, not a tree. I am a man. But what is it to be that? Like every other being, I am a splinter of the infinite deity, but I cannot contrast myself with any animal, any plant or any stone. Only a mythical being has a range greater than man's. How then can a man form any definite opinions about himself?

We are a psychic process which we do not control, or only partly direct. Consequently, we cannot have any final judgment about ourselves or our lives. If we had, we would know everything – but at most that is only a pretence. At bottom we never know how it has all come about. The story of a life begins somewhere, at some particular point we happen to remember; and even then it was already highly complex. We do not know how life is going to turn out. Therefore the story has no beginning, and the end can only be vaguely hinted at.

The life of man is a dubious experiment. It is a tremendous phenomenon only in numerical terms. Individually, it is so fleeting, so insufficient, that it is literally a miracle that anything can exist and develop at all. I was impressed by that fact long ago, as a young medical student, and it seemed to me miraculous that I should not have been prematurely annihilated.

Life has always seemed to me like a plant that lives on its rhizome. Its true life is invisible, hidden in the rhizome. The part that appears above ground lasts only a single summer. Then it withers away – an ephemeral apparition. When we think of the unending growth and decay of life and civilisations, we cannot escape the impression of absolute nullity. Yet I have never lost a sense of something that lives and endures underneath the eternal flux. What we see is the blossom, which passes. The rhizome remains.

In the end the only events in my life worth telling are those when the imperishable world irrupted into this transitory one. That is why I speak chiefly of inner experiences, amongst which I include my dreams and visions. These form the *prima materia* of my scientific work. They were the fiery magma out of which the stone that had to be worked was crystallised.

All other memories of travels, people and my surroundings have paled beside these interior happenings. Many people have participated in the story of our times and written about it; if the reader wants an account of that, let him turn to them or get somebody to tell it to him. Recollection of the outward events of my life has largely faded or disappeared. But my encounters with the 'other' reality, my bouts with the unconscious, are indelibly engraved upon my memory. In that realm there has always been wealth in abundance, and everything else has lost importance by comparison.

Similarly, other people are established inalienably in my memories only if their names were entered in the scrolls of my destiny from the beginning, so that encountering them was at the same time a kind of recollection.

Inner experiences also set their seal on the outward events that came my way and assumed importance for me in youth or later on. I early arrived at the insight that when no answer comes from within to the problems and complexities of life, they ultimately mean very little. Outward circumstances are no substitute for inner experience. Therefore my life has been singularly poor in outward happenings. I cannot tell much about them, for it would strike me as hollow and insubstantial. I can understand myself only in the light of inner happenings. It is these that make up the singularity of my life, and with these my autobiography deals.

C.G. Jung
Memories, Dreams, Reflections

At times I was afraid, not only of the situation in which I found myself but also of the inner journey. I felt that I could be lost and wander into madness as a way of escaping the pain of self-examination. At the same time I was possessed by a burning desire to find and understand truth and discover my own centre. Bede Griffiths, a Roman Catholic Benedictine monk, went to India in 1955 and assisted in the founding of an ashram, a place of prayer and meditation, which became an important location for encounter between East and West. He has written about the quest for the centre and I recall his book, *Return to the Centre* . . .

The whole question is, what is the true Self? What is the true Centre of man's being? Is it the ego, making itself independent, seeking to be master of the world, or is there an 'I' beyond this, a deeper Centre of personal being, which is grounded in the Truth, which is one with the universal Self, the Law of the universe? This is the great discovery of Indian thought, the discovery of the Self, the Atman, the Ground of personal being, which is one with the Brahman, the Ground of universal being. It is not reached by thought; on the contrary, it is only reached by transcending thought. Reason, like the self of which it is the faculty, has to transcend itself. As long as it remains turned towards the senses, to the material world, it will always remain defective, unable to discover the Truth. But the moment it turns inwards to its Source and knows itself in its Ground by a pure intuition, then it knows the truth of its own being and the being of the world, and then it becomes really free. 'You will know the truth, and the truth will make you free.' This is redemption, to be set free from the senses and the material world and to discover their Ground and Source in the Self, which is the Word of God within. The Fall of Man is the fall from this Ground, this Centre of freedom and immortality, into subjection to the senses and this material world, and Reason is the serpent. Reason can either be subject to the eternal Law, the universal Reason, and then it becomes Wisdom, it knows the Self, or it can seek to be the master of the world, and then it becomes demonic. It is the demon of the modern world. In every generation the Fall of Man is repeated, but never, perhaps, on a wider scale than today.

How then to recover from the Fall, how to return to the Centre? This is the problem of the modern world, but it has been the problem of the world from the beginning. Every ancient culture, as Mircea Eliade has shown, built its life round such a Centre. It might be a building, a temple, a city, or simply the home; it might be a place – a mountain, a grove, a burial ground; or it might be a person – a priest or king or seer. But always it was a point where contact could be made with the Source of being. It was a point where heaven and earth converge, where human life is open to the infinite Transcendence. This was the essential thing, to keep contact with the Transcendent, so that human life did not become closed on itself. But the modern world has removed every such point of contact. Everything has become profane, that is, outside the sphere of the holy. Temple and palace, priest and king, sacred grove and mountain, all must be abolished, so that the world of nature and the world of man alike may be emptied of a transcendent significance, of any ultimate meaning. No wonder that there is a rebellion among the young against this drab, one-dimensional world. Young people now come to India from the West, seeking to recover the sense of the sacred, the inner meaning of life, which has been lost in the West. But India too is losing it rapidly. Wherever modern civilization spreads, all holiness, all sense of the sacred, all awareness of a transcendent Reality disappears. This is just another Fall of Man.

Bede Griffiths
Return to the Centre

As I write these words at our house in the Suffolk countryside I have just said goodbye to a friend who is setting out to walk across the Sahara. I regard him as one of the last of the 'gentleman' travellers. As a young man he travelled in the party of the formidable Freya Stark. According to my friend, she was not over-impressed with him and, to his amusement, recorded that fact in one of her books.

I have travelled through parts of the Sahara, across Namibia and Botswana and through the desert regions of Uganda. The desert fascinates me and I can understand why individuals have gained spiritual insight in such places. In the desert, as at sea, one knows what it is to be vulnerable.

Carlo Carretto held a powerful position within 'Catholic Action' in Italy and gave up his post to join the followers of Charles de Foucauld known as the Little Brothers of Jesus. It was in the desert that he learned important lessons about prayer and recorded something of that experience in a series of letters later made into a book and entitled, *Letters from the Desert*. He echoes so many of my own feelings. When I lay awake at night attempting to make sense of what was happening to me and finding little comfort in my faith, I remembered his words about darkness. Wisdom does not come cheaply and the things of God must not be treated lightly.

When I first came to the Sahara I was afraid of the night.

For some, night means more work, for others dissipation, for still others insomnia, boredom.

For me now it's quite different. Night is first of all rest, real rest. At sunset a great serenity sets in, as though nature were obeying a sudden sign from God.

The wind which has howled all day ceases, the heat dies down, the atmosphere becomes clear and limpid, and great peace spreads everywhere, as though man and the elements wanted to refresh themselves after the great battle with the day and its sun.

Yes, the night here is different. It has not lost its purity, its mystery. It has remained as God made it, his creation, bringer of good and life.

With your work finished and the caravan halted, you stretch out on the sand with a blanket under your head and breathe in the gentle breeze which has replaced the dry, fiery daytime wind.

Then you leave the camp and go down to the dunes for prayer. Time passes undisturbed. No obligations harass you, no noise disturbs you, no worry awaits you: time is all yours. So you satiate yourself with prayer and silence, while the stars light up in the sky.

Those who have never seen them cannot believe what the stars are like in the desert; the complete absence of artificial light, the vastness of the horizon only seem to increase their number and brightness. It is certainly an unforgettable experience. Only the camp fire with the tea water boiling on top and the bread for supper baking underneath, glows with a mellow light against the sparkling heaven.

Carlo Carretto
Letters from the Desert

My requests for the guards to bring me books continued. One morning after I had returned from the bathroom my guard uttered the magic word 'Tek' (take). I held out my hand to receive whatever he had to give me. It was a book. When the guard had locked the door I removed my blindfold and discovered that he had given me a novel published by Mills and Boon. My heart sank because I knew that it would be read before noon and also because I wanted something more substantial. I read the book thoroughly, however, and it did pass an hour or so. There is a sequel to this story: when I was released I mentioned that the novels published by this house were not my favourite reading. The publisher got to hear of this and, being a good-humoured soul, transposed my portrait on to the cover of a Mills and Boon book called *Reluctant Hostage*. The cover was framed and given to me. It now has pride of place in my study.

The guards must have obtained a small supply of books because the following morning

I received another. This time it was *Remote People* by Evelyn Waugh. In 1930, Waugh visited Abyssinia to attend and report on the coronation of the Emperor, Haile Selassie. Having visited that country several times I found a lot of pleasure in his witty and descriptive writing.

The ceremony was immensely long, even according to the original schedule, and the clergy succeeded in prolonging it by at least an hour and a half beyond the allotted time. The six succeeding days of celebration were to be predominantly military, but the coronation day itself was in the hands of the Church, and they were going to make the most of it. Psalms, canticles, and prayers succeeded each other, long passages of Scripture were read, all in the extinct ecclesiastical tongue, Ghiz. Candles were lit one by one; the coronation oaths were proposed and sworn; the diplomats shifted uncomfortably in their gilt chairs, noisy squabbles broke out round the entrance between the imperial guard and the retainers of the local chiefs. Professor W., who was an expert of high transatlantic reputation on Coptic ritual, occasionally remarked: 'They are beginning the Mass now,' 'That was the offertory,' 'No, I was wrong; it was the consecration,' 'No, I was wrong; I think it is the secret Gospel,' 'No, I think it must be the Epistle,' 'How very curious; I don't believe it was a Mass at all,' '*Now* they *are* beginning the Mass . . .' and so on. Presently the bishops began to fumble among the band-boxes, and investiture began. At long intervals the Emperor was presented with robe, orb, spurs, spear, and finally with the crown. A salute of guns was fired, and the crowds outside, scattered all over the surrounding waste spaces, began to cheer; the imperial horses reared up, plunged on top of each other, kicked the gilding off the front of the coach, and broke their traces. The coachman sprang from the box and whipped them from a safe distance. Inside the pavilion there was a general sense of relief; it had all been very fine and impressive, now for a cigarette, a drink, and a change into less formal costume. Not a bit of it. The next thing was to crown the Empress and the heir apparent; another salvo of guns followed, during which an Abyssinian groom had two ribs broken in an attempt to unharness a pair of the imperial horses. Again we felt for our hats and gloves. But the Coptic choir still sang; the bishops then proceeded to take back the regalia with proper prayers, lections, and canticles.

'I have noticed some very curious variations in the Canon of the Mass,' remarked the professor, 'particularly with regard to the kiss of peace.'

Then the Mass began.

For the first time throughout the morning the Emperor and Empress left their thrones; they disappeared behind the

curtains into the improvised sanctuary;
most of the clergy went too. The stage
was empty save for the diplomats; their
faces were set and strained, their attitudes
inelegant. I have seen just that look in
crowded railway carriages, at dawn, between Avignon and Marseilles. Their
clothes made them funnier still. Marshal
d'Esperez alone preserved his dignity, his
chest thrown out, his baton poised on his
knee, rigid as a war memorial, and, as far as
one could judge, wide awake.

It was now about eleven o'clock, the time
at which the emperor was due to leave the
pavilion. Punctually to plan, three Abyssinian aeroplanes rose to greet him. They
circled round and round over the tent,
eagerly demonstrating their newly acquired art by swooping and curvetting
within a few feet of the canvas roof. The
noise was appalling; the local chiefs stirred
in their sleep and rolled on to their faces;
only by the opening and closing of their lips

and the turning of their music could we discern that the Coptic deacons were still singing.

'A most unfortunate interruption. I missed many of the verses,' said the professor.

Eventually, at about half-past twelve, the Mass came to an end, and the Emperor and Empress, crowned, shuffling along under a red and gold canopy and looking, as Irene remarked, exactly like the processional statues of Seville, crossed to a grand stand, from which the Emperor delivered a royal proclamation; an aeroplane scattered copies of the text and, through loud speakers, the Court heralds re-read it to the populace.

There was a slightly ill-tempered scramble among the photographers and cinema-men – I received a heavy blow in the middle of the back from a large camera, and a hoarse rebuke, 'Come along there now – let the eyes of the world see.'

Dancing broke out once more among the clergy, and there is no knowing how long things might not have gone on, had not the photographers so embarrassed and jostled them, and outraged their sense of reverence, that they withdrew to finish their devotions alone in the cathedral.

Then at last the Emperor and Empress were conducted to their coach and borne off to luncheon by its depleted but still demonstratively neurasthenic team of horses.

Evelyn Waugh
'Remote People'

NATURALLY enough my guards were most concerned about their own security. They knew that Beirut was under constant observation by satellite and there were many who would be anxious to discover details of where hostages were kept. They were also worried that the building would be stormed, and kept a large cache of weapons on hand. I am quite convinced that, had there been an attempt to free me, the guards would have had no hesitation in shooting me and dying themselves in the ensuing battle.

With this in mind, I read *The Blue Nile* by Alan Moorhead. He recounts how the Victorians dealt with a case of hostage-taking in Abyssinia.

A predecessor of Haile Selassie was holding the British Envoy Rassam and others. General Napier came straight to the point in his letter to Theodore . . .

'To Theodorus, King of Abyssinia.
'I am commanded by Her Majesty
the Queen of England to demand that

the prisoners whom your Majesty has wrongly detained in captivity shall be immediately released and sent in safety to the British Camp.

'Should your Majesty fail to comply with this command, I am further commanded to enter your Majesty's country at the head of an army to enforce it, and nothing will arrest my progress until this object shall have been accomplished.

'My Sovereign has no desire to deprive you of any part of your dominions, nor to subvert your authority, although it is obvious that such would in all probability be the result of hostilities.

'Your Majesty might avert this danger by immediate surrender of the prisoners. But should they not be delivered safely into my hands, should they suffer a continuance of ill-treatment, or should any injury befall

them, your Majesty will be held
personally responsible, and no hope of
further condonation need be entertained.
R. Napier, Lt.-General,
Commander-in-Chief,
Bombay Army.'

It was a fine martial declaration, but it is
doubtful if it would have had much influ-
ence on Theodore even if it had ever reached
him. As things happened it fell into rebel
hands and was delivered to Rassam in
Magdala, who immediately destroyed it,
fearing that it would enrage Theodore
against the prisoners. Napier's second com-
munication, a proclamation to the people of
Ethiopia, which was also issued about this
time, was much more effective:

'To the Governors, the Chiefs, the
Religious Orders, and the People of
Abyssinia.
    'It is known to you that Theodorus
King of Abyssinia detains in captivity

the British Consul Cameron, the British
Envoy Rassam, and many others, in
violation of the laws of all civilized
nations. All friendly persuasion having
failed to obtain their release, my
Sovereign has commanded me to lead
an army to liberate them.

'All who befriend the prisoners or
assist in their liberation shall be
rewarded, but those who may injure
them shall be severely punished.

'When the time shall arrive for the
march of a British Army through your
country, bear in mind, people of
Abyssinia, that the Queen of England
has no unfriendly feeling towards you,
and no design against your country or
your liberty. Your religious
establishments, your persons and your
property shall be carefully protected. All
supplies required for my soldiers shall
be paid for; no peaceable inhabitant
shall be molested.

'The sole object for which the British force has been sent to Abyssinia is the liberation of Her Majesty's servants and others unjustly detained as captives, and as soon as that object is effected it will be withdrawn. There is no intention to occupy permanently any portion of the Abyssinian territory, or to interfere with the Government of the country.'

Alan Moorhead
The Blue Nile

As I exercised my own memory and attempted to keep a day-to-day diary in my head I thought back to the published diaries I had read during my life. Many years ago I spent some weeks convalescing at Osborne House in the Isle of Wight. This former royal residence is now partly a museum and partly a convalescent home. In the last century it was a favourite retreat for Queen Victoria and it was at Osborne that I first came across the collected letters and journals of the queen. Although they have been carefully edited they do make entertaining reading. In Cambridge I discovered several volumes on the famous market bookstall and promptly snapped them up. The following extract by the late queen describes an incident which might well have brought her reign to an abrupt end.

18th Aug. 1875 – This has been an eventful day, and one of terrible and undying recollections! At half past five left dear Osborne, with Beatrice and Leopold, and embarked at

Trinity Pier. The evening was very fine, so bright, and no wind. The *Victoria and Albert* followed us. When we neared Stokes Bay, Beatrice said, very calmly, 'Mama, there is a yacht coming against us,' and I saw the tall masts and large sails of a schooner looming over us. In an instant came an awful, most terrifying crash, accompanied by a very severe shake and reel. Horatia [Stopford] and Harriet [Phipps] came running and saying there had been a collision, and at the same time General Ponsonby and Lord Bridport rushed up saying, 'There is no danger.' Then only a frightful alarm seized me, lest some of our people, who always stand in the bows of the vessel, might get hurt. I was assured, however, they were all safe, and Leopold came round at the same moment, so that I knew nothing had happened to him.

It all took only a few seconds, and, when I enquired to whom the yacht belonged, I was told she had gone down! In great distress I said, 'Take everyone, take everyone on board,' repeating this several times. I then went forward, to where all the excitement had been going on, and was horrified to find not a single vestige of the yacht, merely a few spars and deck chairs floating about. Two boats were moving round, and we saw one of our men swimming about with a life-belt, and one poor man in the water, who was pulled into the barge, nearly drowned, with his face quite black. I saw no others in the water, but on deack three or four yachtsmen, also a lady, looking anxiously from one side to the other. These had jumped across from the sinking yacht on to the *Alberta*. At first it was hoped that everyone had been saved, and General Ponsonby said the numbers were being counted. Alas! then it became clear that one lady, whom Leopold had distinctly seen on the deck with the other, was missing, also one man – a dreadful moment.

I was asked to leave the forepart of the ship, as two poor men were being brought up, and the sight was very distressing. However, from near the paddle wheel I could see the poor man being lifted out of the water and lying on the deck, with his coat cut off and his face perfectly black, Dr. McEwan and two sailors bending over him and moving his arms backwards and forwards. But he gave no sign of life. He was the Captain or Master of the *Mistletoe*, as the yacht was called, a big man of at least seventy. The other, whom I had not noticed before, turned out to be Mr. Heywood, the owner. He also was insensible, but it was hoped he would do well. The poor Captain had probably been injured by a blow, and it was feared he could not be brought round. We saw one of the yachtsmen holding his arm in great agony. It was broken, and no one could attend to him properly, as the doctor was so occupied with the poor old man. It was now discovered that the poor young lady, who was on board, was the sister of the one who was drowned, and

Mr. Heywood was the brother-in-law, whose wife was at Ryde, from whence they had been sailing. Commander Fullerton, of the *Victoria and Albert*, had jumped overboard most gallantly, just as he was, only removing his sword, and had hurt his hand in trying to save the poor lady, who had slipped from his grasp! Lieutenant Britten and two sailors had also been in the water. Commander Fullerton and one of our men had actually gone down with the sinking yacht, and had been saved with difficulty. But the poor lady, it is too awful, and I cannot get over it. Harriet had gone off at once to the distraught sister who stood at the end of the vessel, the picture of calm, silent despair, unable to shed a tear. She and the dying man were most harrowing scenes, which as well as the crash, shock, and the complete disappearance of the yacht, will never be forgotten by any of us who were present!

In vain they searched, *no* sign or trace of the poor missing one was to be seen, and so we had to go on finally, having first cut off part of the rigging of the unfortunate *Mistletoe*, which had got entangled on the *Alberta*, whose bowsprit had been carried away. The poor young lady's name was Peel. She was told she might go below to see her brother-in-law, who was recovering, and this was a great comfort to her. The poor old man was dying, in fact I fear already dead. When Miss Peel had come up again I went to say a few words of truest sympathy to her, and pressed her hand. She could only murmur a few words of thanks, and her expression of grief was heart-rending to see.

The Letters of Queen Victoria
(Second Series)

TRANSLATIONS of the historians Thucydides and Herodotus both found their way to me. The latter enlivened his script with the gossip of the market place, which makes for good reading even if professional historians might regard it as suspect. Herodotus, writing in the fifth century BC was a prodigious traveller and as he journeyed he collected information on Egypt, Syria, Libya, Italy and Sicily, among many other places.

The following extract from his *History of the Greek and Persian War* is a good example of how entertaining a writer he could be.

Concerning Egypt itself I shall extend my remarks to a great length, because there is no country that possesses so many wonders, nor any that has such a number of works which defy description. Not only is the climate different from that of the rest of the world, and the rivers unlike any other rivers, but the people also, in most of their manners and customs, exactly reverse the common practice of mankind. The women attend the markets and trade, while the men sit at home at the loom; and here, while the rest of the world works the woof up the warp, the Egyptians work it down; the women likewise carry burdens upon their shoulders, while the men carry them upon their heads; the women urinate standing, the men crouching. They eat their food out of doors in the streets, but retire for the purpose of defecating to their houses, giving as a reason that what is unseemly, but necessary, ought to be done in secret, but what has nothing unseemly about it, should be done openly. A woman cannot serve the priestly office, either for god or goddess, but men are priests to both; sons need not support their parents unless they choose, but daughters must, whether they choose or no.

In other countries the priests have long hair, in Egypt their heads are shaven; elsewhere it is customary, in mourning, for near relations to cut their hair close: the Egyptians, who wear no hair at any other time, when they lose a relative, let their beards and the hair of their heads grow long. All other men pass their lives separate from animals, the Egyptians have animals always living with them; others make barley and wheat their food; it is a disgrace to do so in Egypt, where the grain they live on is spelt, which some call *zea*. Dough they knead with their feet; but they mix mud, and even take up dung, with their hands. They are the only people in the world – they at least, and such as have learned the practice from them – who use circumcision. Their men wear two garments apiece, their women but one. They put on the rings and fasten the ropes to sails inside; others put them outside. When they write or calculate, instead of going, like the Greeks, from left to right, they move their hand from right to left; and they insist, notwithstanding, that it is they who go to the right, and the Greeks who go wrong. They have two quite different kinds of writing, one of which is called sacred, the other common.

Herodotus
The Second Book

ALTHOUGH I have been a lifelong Anglican, the Orthodox Church has provided me with a second home. As a young student of theology, I would often slip away to attend a service at the Russian Orthodox Cathedral in London. The unique mixture of order and freedom within the liturgy has its own special appeal. In the main, the congregation remain standing. There are seats by the wall – hence the saying, 'The weakest go to the wall'. The service is conducted with considerable respect for order and form and yet the members of the congregation have a lot of freedom while it is in progress. Some remain virtually immobile – others move to light a candle or to pray before an icon. Within the Orthodox liturgy there is the opportunity for participation at many different levels: throughout it all one is conscious of the great mystery that is God and this awareness produces a sense of awe and respect.

To many, Orthodox belief and practice is a total mystery. In 1963, Timothy Ware (now

Bishop Kallistos Ware) published *The Orthodox Church* for the general reader. It continues to be well worth attention as it gives a good overview of the history of Orthodoxy and a clear account of its faith and worship. In an age where limited value is placed on history and tradition the Orthodox Church has much to contribute.

> True Orthodox fidelity to the past must always be a *creative* fidelity; for true Orthodoxy can never rest satisfied with a barren 'theology of repetition', which, parrot-like, repeats accepted formulae without striving to understand what lies behind them. Loyalty to Tradition, properly understood, is not something mechanical, a dull process of handing down what has been received. An Orthodox thinker must see Tradition *from within*, he must enter into its inner spirit. In order to live within Tradition, it is not enough simply to give intellectual assent to a system of doctrine; for Tradition is far more than a set of abstract propositions

– it is a life, a personal encounter with Christ in the Holy Spirit. Tradition is not only kept by the Church – it lives in the Church, it is the life of the Holy Spirit in the Church. The Orthodox conception of Tradition is not static but dynamic, not a dead acceptance of the past but a living experience of the Holy Spirit in the present. Tradition, while inwardly changeless (for God does not change), is constantly assuming new forms, which supplement the old without superseding them. Orthodox often speak as if the period of doctrinal formulation were wholly at an end, yet this is not the case. Perhaps in our own day new Ecumenical Councils will meet, and Tradition will be enriched by fresh statements of the faith.

This idea of Tradition as a living thing has been well expressed by Georges Florovsky:

Tradition is the witness of the Spirit; the Spirit's unceasing revelation and preaching of good tidings . . . To accept and understand Tradition we must live within the Church, we must be conscious of the grace-giving presence of the Lord in it; we must feel the breath of the Holy Ghost in it . . . Tradition is not only a protective, conservative principle; it is, primarily, the principle of growth and regeneration . . . Tradition is the constant abiding of the Spirit and not only the memory of words.

Tradition is the witness of the Spirit: in the words of Christ, 'When the Spirit of truth has come, he will guide you into all truth' (John 16:13). It is this divine promise that forms the basis of the Orthodox devotion to Tradition.

Timothy Ware
The Orthodox Church

JUST before returning to the Middle East in January 1987, I attended the Christmas liturgy at the Russian Orthodox church in Kensington. It was packed and little did I realise that this was the last Church service I would be attending for almost five years. When I returned home at the end of 1991, I went back to the church for a Sunday morning liturgy. At the end, the congregation gathered around their bishop, Anthony of Sourozh, to listen to his homily. When he had finished he turned towards me and said, 'Welcome home. We have never forgotten you. Now we shall all sing for you.' The congregation sang as only an Orthodox congregation can sing. The music spoke of a state in which joy, sorrow and mystery combine in harmony to produce a profound sense of peace.

As we were leaving the church and I was receiving the embraces of the congregation, someone drew me aside. 'You were here at Christmas just before you disappeared?' I nodded my head. 'I remember,' she said.

'I remember in particular because that very morning also in the congregation was Irina Ratushinskaya. She had just been released. You were about to be captured.'

Irina Ratushinskaya, a writer and poet of distinction, was twenty-eight years old when she was imprisoned in the Soviet Union because of her writing. Her book *Grey is the Colour of Hope* tells her story and we join the writer in a railway carriage with other prisoners on their way to prison camp.

In the carriage, the fact that I am a 'political' arouses much interest. I have to explain everything from scratch yet again: about human rights, about my poetry, then read that poetry – to the whole carriage. The guard is clearly interested, too, for he makes no move to stop me. Nowadays, since my arrival in the West, people frequently express surprise at my ability to recite from memory, and at the ease with which I answer questions. The reason for this, ladies and gentlemen, is that my first large audiences – a hundred people or more – were crammed into these carriages, where not everyone could see me, just hear my voice. The poetry had to be read in as straightforward a manner as possible, and the questions answered simply, without trying to be 'clever', just as I do now in English, for my knowledge of English is no more sophisticated than the 'ordinary' Russian of my fellow prisoners. There may be the odd few in the camps who can recite the verses of Omar Khayyám, but the overwhelming majority of camp inmates are semi-literate. Nevertheless, I recite:

I see a household cat in my despairing,
Who makes no noise and knows how to
    behave.
Her needs are few – a scratch will start her
    purring,
A scrap to eat and whispered words: 'Be
    brave!'

My throat escapes her claws' unlooked-for
    pricking,
She never interferes if I have guests.
The minute-hand enchants her with its
    ticking
And brings her consolation, even rest.
She climbs up on my knee when sensing
    nightfall,
And, childlike, noses round and falls asleep
As on my book I see the patterned light fall,
Those meaningless cast-iron shadows creep.
But in the darkness, like a mouse a-chewing,
She stirs as if in sleep she seemed to see
A dwelling that sets off her tiny mewing,
The house of warmth that you will build
    for me.

I read on: what price I and my poems if I can't
get through to this audience? Too many of us
have been too far 'removed from the people'
already. I recite whatever comes to mind: the
poem about the unattainable cherry-red
dress, the one about the exemplary

Motherland, who executes the best of her children, the one about the flying cat . . .

Granny Tonia weeps again. After blowing her nose, she fishes out a wrinkled apple from somewhere. 'Here, daughter, you have it, you're young. I'm not going to come out of the camp alive, anyway, but you'll live. You keep writing!'

I accept the apple, my first honorarium, still warm from her hands. I'll keep writing, Granny Tonia. If I survive, I'll write. Actually, sentimentality exacts a just price, like any tendency to paint something in one colour. The prison administration tries to reduce every prisoner to grey, and it would be equally wrong for me to depict the same in rosy hues. While Granny Tonia and I were succumbing to sentiment, someone stole my toothbrush out of my bag, and it would be silly for me to be surprised by that.

Irina Ratushinskaya
Grey is the Colour of Hope

YEAR after year I sat in my room listening to the frightening noise of battle outside. There is a strange irony in the way that this 'Holy Land' has been the scene of so much unholy activity down the ages. I had endless time to ponder this and also to reflect on suffering which has so terribly afflicted the people of this region for generations. A number of years ago I came across the diaries of Etty Hillesum. Etty was born in Holland and just before the outbreak of war moved to Amsterdam. Ominously she was Jewish by birth although she claimed no strong religious affiliation. During the terrible years from 1941 to 1943 she went voluntarily with the trapped Jews to a camp at Westerbork during which she kept a remarkable diary. This moving document, written in twelve exercise books, breaks off in September 1942 when she was deported to Auschwitz. On 30 November 1942 Etty Hillesum died. She was twenty-nine years old. Her words are for everyone regardless of race, tribe or religion.

I know and share the many sorrows and sad circumstances that a human being can experience, but I do not cling to them, I do not prolong such moments of agony. They pass through me, like life itself, as a broad, eternal stream, they become part of that stream, and life continues. And as a result all my strength is preserved, does not become tagged on to futile sorrow or rebelliousness.

Ought we not, from time to time, open ourselves up to cosmic sadness? One day I shall surely be able to say to Ilse Blumenthal, 'Yes, life is beautiful, and I value it anew at the end of every day, even though I know that the sons of mothers, and you are one such mother, are being murdered in concentration camps. And you must be able to bear your sorrow; even if it seems to crush you, you will be able to stand up again, for human beings are so strong, and your sorrow must become an integral part of yourself, part of your body and your soul, you mustn't run away from it, but bear it like an adult. Do not relieve your feelings through hatred, do not seek to be avenged on all German mothers, for they, too, sorrow at this very moment for their slain and murdered sons. Give your sorrow all the space and shelter in itself that it is due, for if everyone bears his grief honestly and courageously, the sorrow that now fills the world will abate. But if you do not clear a decent shelter for your sorrow, and instead reserve most of the space inside you for hatred and thoughts of revenge – from which new sorrows will be born for others – then sorrow will never cease in this world and will multiply. And if you have given sorrow the space its gentle origins demand, then you may truly say: life is beautiful and so rich. So beautiful and so rich that it makes you want to believe in God.'

An Interrupted Life
The Diaries of Etty Hillesum

WHEN my spirits faltered I would think back to the people who had encouraged me by the way in which they had coped under acute pressure. One such was my friend Bishop Desmond Tutu. In 1982, Archbishop Runcie had sent me to South Africa to give support to Bishop Desmond when he was secretary to the South African Council of Churches and he and the Council were subject to an investigation by the government of the day. The hope was to discredit and silence both bishop and Council. The Eloff Commission of Inquiry was set up and Desmond was 'invited' to present himself for questioning and make a statement. I was present for some of the time and found the experience unpleasant and not a little frightening. I listened to Desmond as he spoke before Mr Justice Eloff and his fellow commissioners.

As I read the address again, I can hear him speaking out of a tradition that extends way beyond South Africa and finds its origin in the prophets of the Old Testament.

If we are to say that religion cannot be concerned with politics then we are really saying that there is a substantial part of human life in which God's writ does not run. If it is not God's then whose is it? Who is in charge if not the God and Father of Our Lord Jesus Christ?

On the Church and politics we could say much, much more. Is it not interesting just how often people and churches are accused of mixing religion with politics? – almost always whenever they condemn a particular social political dispensation as being unjust. If the South African Council of Churches were to say now that it thought apartheid was not so bad, I am as certain as anything that we would not be finding ourselves where we are today. Why is it not being political for a religious body or a religious leader to praise a social political dispensation?

I need to point out that in the Old Testament God was first experienced by the Israelites in the event of the Exodus. That was how they came into contact with God. They were at the time just a rabble of slaves. They did not encounter God in some religious event such as a sacrifice or at worship; He revealed Himself in helping them to escape from bondage, and what could be more political than helping captives to escape? And it is this political event of the Exodus which becomes the founding event of the people of God. It becomes the paradigmatic event of the Bible, so that, looking at what God did in the Exodus, they extrapolate backwards and say that a God who did so and so, must clearly be the God, the Lord of creation; and they can extrapolate forwards and say that a God who can choose a people in this way, must be a God who has a purpose for them, and that is why we said at the beginning that God has taken human history seriously, unlike the nature gods. And when God redeemed us in Our Lord and Saviour Jesus

Christ, it was not through a religious event. No, it was through an act of execution, used against common criminals, a judicial event that would be sanctioned, not by the ecclesiastical leaders, but by the political ruler in Judea.

I want to quote some strange words. I will explain afterwards where they come from, M'Lord. I start on paragraph 2 and the heading is *Rest in the Status Quo*:

The other extreme however is still more fatal to the Church's effective witness to the world, and that is acquiescence in unjust conditions. Silence may never be kept about the social implications of the Gospel of Christ. There can be little doubt that the present low level of the spiritual life is in no small measure due to the dilution of the eternal principles. The whole Church longs and prays for a revival, but is it psychologically sound to expect enthusiastic, joyful spiritual life among those living in misery, hunger and privation? Moses and Aaron also claimed to quicken new hope and courage in the hearts of their enslaved people, but what do we read in Exodus 6:8? But they did not listen to Moses on account of the despondency and cruel bondage.

The Charge against the Church: The strongest charge against the Church is born exactly out of the conception of many that she has not grieved over the ruin of Joseph, but acquiesced in this in the conditions of injustice, exploitation and coercion. The Evangelical Lutheran Church in 1931 made a survey in a vast suburb of Berlin among a thousand former members who had left the Church. Not one of them recorded objections against the doctrines of the Church as a reason for cessation. The great charge was that the Church had no eye or ear for justice or for the oppressed. The Church identified only with those on the sunny side of life, who pledged their support; not high moral ideals, but self-interest dominated its attitude. The Church was on the side of the vested interest of ruling classes. Instead of rebuking or condemning their despotism and injustice, she admonished the poor and oppressed to be docile, to bear their hard burden patiently, to hope for better conditions in the hereafter, to suffer the ills of the present in order to receive the heaven of the future. Our Church in South Africa must honestly face the charges brought against her. She is too much inclined to demand support and respect of members on account of past services to the people. The city labourer wants more than this. The past leaves him cold. He wants to know what the Church does for him here and now. In former years the reverence in respect of which the Church was regarded, silenced her members even though they differed from her, but now the city dweller is much more critically inclined, and he is more candid to air his grievances. One of the most hopeful signs in our cities is that the Church is so close to the working classes. Today she is almost exclusively supported by the working classes. Today she is almost exclusively supported by the labourer, by the low paid person. These constitute her office bearers and her best members . . .

After further quotation, Bishop Tutu went on to say:

That is not a statement by the SACC. It is a statement made by the Dutch Reformed Church, published in a book entitled *Kerk en Stad*. It was in preparation for the Volkskongres in July 1947. It is quoted from a paper that was delivered by

Dominee Dawid Botha, the Moderator of the Sendigkerk. The paper, 'The Kingdom of God and the Churches in South Africa', was delivered at the National Conference of the SACC in 1980

Desmond Tutu
Hope and Suffering

ALTHOUGH books were now arriving in dribs and drabs, more often than not they were lightweight romantic novels. It was clearly impossible for the guards to go out and buy specific titles and I puzzled as to how to persuade them to bring me books of any substance. Then I had an idea. One day a guard who was reasonably friendly came into my cell. I repeated my usual plea for reading material and told him that the novels he was bringing were better than nothing but very quickly read. I asked him if he would let me use a pencil and paper for a moment. He produced both and as carefully as I could I drew a picture of a penguin. 'Look,' I said. 'If you see that on the front of a book, buy it. It will be a good book.' 'What you call?' he asked. 'Penguin,' I said, 'Penguin Books'. He took back the pencil and paper and left the cell. Several days later he returned and uttered the familiar command, 'Tek'. A book was placed in my hand and when he left the room I discovered, to my great delight, that it was a Penguin. Thereafter I received a regular supply.

Among the Penguins I received was a familiar friend. In the 1930s Laurie Lee set out from his home in the Cotswolds with his violin to seek his fortune. *As I Walked out one Midsummer Morning* records his adventures. It was a lovely book to read again and enabled me to travel far and wide in imagination while trapped in a dark damp room.

This extract describes Laurie Lee's encounter with the South African poet Roy Campbell, who was then living in Toledo.

I stayed with the Campbells for about a week, and was treated with a matter-of-fact kindness which surprised and charmed me. I'd arrived from nowhere, but nobody bothered me with questions; I was simply accepted and given the run of the house.

During most of the daylight hours Roy lay low and slept, appearing at nightfall like some ruffled sea-bird, leaning against a pillar with his arms stretched wide as though drying his salt-wet wings. One saw him gathering his wits in great gulps of breath, after which he would be ready for anything.

Mary and little Anna lived in an intimate calm of their own, quietly busy with their spiritual chores, and could be seen in the morning going off to Mass, veiled and modest as shadows, and so native in appearance that when I met them in the street I often forgot and addressed them in Spanish. When they returned from their devotions they would come back transformed, light-footed and chirpy with gossip, their early silence now swept away, and their eyes sparkling, as though they'd been to a party.

One evening, to keep my hand in, I played for an hour in the streets and made over seven pesetas, in copper. I carried it back to the house and poured it out on the table, to the delight of the astonished girls. We bought a few litres of wine and went up on to the roof, where there was a terrace with a view of the city. It was still light, and the humped little red-tiled houses, scaled and patchy, clustered around us like crabs.

We ate supper and drank, and as the evening darkened, Roy coughed and began to sing, croaking the corny laments and border ballads that were near to his expatriate heart. His voice was blurred as usual, and rough as a sailor's, yet deeply charged with feeling; more than that, he sang with a poet's care, renewing the worn, familiar words. 'Scots Wa Hae', 'The Bonnie Earl of Murray', sounded as if they'd just been written – with the blood of the slain still wet. To me, until then, they'd just been songs of the schoolroom, now I heard them fresh and bitter, while Roy sat with hunched shoulders, rocking backwards and forwards, often at the point of tears.

Suddenly the maid, from somewhere down in the house, hearing his singing, started up too – not a brash interruption, but like a night-bird answering to the husky call of another. Sad Castilian airs, harsh but haunting, came floating up the well of the stairs. Each new song from Roy would call up another from the girl, rising like bubbles of grief in the darkness, not clashing with his but hovering round the edges, offering a compassionate echo.

Later, the night grew cold, and we huddled under furs and blankets, talking till nearly dawn. Summer lightning and shooting stars lit up the Toledo sky with little soundless conflagrations, flickering across the Cathedral and over the faces of the poet and his wife like ripples of phosphorescence.

Laurie Lee
*As I Walked out one Midsummer
Morning*

TRAVEL books have always fascinated me and they understandably had a particular appeal when it was impossible for me to go anywhere other than in my imagination.

I had not heard about Ann Davison until her book, *Last Voyage*, found its way to my prison. She was the first woman to sail single-handed from England to America, and before that she and her husband Frank had led a life full of adventure. He owned an airport. She became a joy-ride pilot. They managed a smallholding and later reared goats on a Scottish island in Loch Lomond. When their various ventures crashed, they decided to sail around the world in a seventy-foot fishing vessel. They started to renovate the ship and when the money ran out they put to sea illegally. After a terrible journey, they find themselves off Portland Bill and tragedy strikes . . .

The current took us into the very centre of Portland Race. The sea was white with insensate rage. Towering pinnacles of water rushed hither and yon, dashing into one another to burst with a shrapnel of foam – or to merge and grow enormous.

From the level of the sea itself it was as the wrath of God, terrifying to behold.

Seated on the bottomless coracle, filled with wonder and awe, we worked away with the paddles to meet the seas. Bravely the little craft tugged up the precipitous slopes and plunged into the depths. I was thinking I would rather be in her than in a dinghy, when suddenly I was in the sea, underneath the float, looking up through the centre where the water was bright green.

There was time to wonder – Is this drowning? – and – How green the water is from this side – then I surfaced, found I was gripping a lifeline.

The float was swinging uneasily at the bottom of a trough. There was no sign of Frank. Terror-stricken, I shrieked for him at the very top of my voice.

He came up about ten yards away. Swam strongly to the float, still holding his paddle, whereon I realised I had lost mine.

We heaved aboard, and lay athwart the ring, gasping, clinging to the lifelines.

'What did that?' I panted.

'Don't know. This is *not* funny.'

Then we saw my paddle, swung upright and set off in pursuit, chasing it up hill and down stormy dale, but it remained forever out of reach.

Suddenly we were in the water again. Under the float. Green water above.

This time we were slower getting aboard. Took longer to recover. We looked at one another in great fear.

'What do we *do*? How do we fight this?'

The upset was so sudden, happened so quickly, we had no notion as to the cause of it. And that was the frightening part.

Dizzily the float tore up and down, swinging and swaying. Tensely we watched the advance of each white-headed mountain. Frank had lost his paddle in the last upset and we could not even make a pretence of fighting.

Then we were flung into the sea again. And this time saw how it happened. Saw with slow-motion clarity how the float was sucked up under a great overhanging crest, and thrown over backwards in the boiling tumult as the wave broke.

This time it was very hard to get back on to the float.

Frank threw an arm about my shoulders: 'All right?'

'Yes.'

'Good-oh.'

We got right inside the float, crouching on the wooden box with water up to our armpits.

There must be some way of stopping it turning over, I thought.

He shouted: 'LOOK OUT!'

Instinctively I leant forward, head down on the ring to meet what was coming. And we did not turn over. But took the full force of the wave as it exploded upon us.

I found myself shouting: 'That's it. That's it. Lean forward. Head down. That foxes 'em.'

Shivering violently with cold I remembered something once read about the mechanics of shivering and put up a great show of exaggerated shudders, partly to offset the numbing cold, and partly as a manifestation of triumph. Frank smiled wanly.

But the conquest was short-lived. The seas grew worse. Boiled in a white lather all about us. Breaking in endless succession . . . We hardly recovered from the onslaught of one before gasping under the next. The weight of water and shock of cold were stunning. Each time a wave broke over us it was with the effect of an icy plunge, although we were actually crouching in water all the time.

Hours dragged out in immeasurable misery as the sea struck with a sledge-hammer to kill a pair of gnats.

No longer buoyed by the slightest hope of rescue we sank into an apathy of endurance, huddled together, heads on the ring, hands grasping lifelines with the prehensile, immovable grip of the newborn. Or the dying. Passively fighting for the lives which were a little less living after every blow.

In a comparative lull, from a wave-top, I glimpsed land, Portland Bill, thin and attenuated in the distance. Pointed to it. Frank slowly stood up and called in a whisper for help.

It was such a pitiful travesty of his usual stentorian bellow I was inexpressibly shocked, and with a surge of protective energy reached up to pull him down, dreading a recurrence of the horror of the other night. Then I saw it was not that . . . and looked wildly round for help. But there was none.

He did not speak. He put out a hand, pressed mine, reassuringly. Smiled at me.

And gradually, the smile fixed and

meaningless and terrible, faded into unconsciousness, into a slow delirium when, blank-eyed, he tried to climb out of the float. I held on to him and feebly tried to rub his hands, my own unfeeling.

A monster wave rose above the rest. Fury piled on fury. Curling, foaming crest. Sweeping down on us. Inescapable. I threw an arm round Frank, leant forward.

The little float drove into the wall of water and was lost within it.

When it broke free Frank was dead.

I stared at the edge of the ring. At the ropes intertwined about it. At the froth and bubbles on the water.

Nothing mattered now. No point in trying any more. The fight was over. I laid my head on my arms and closed my eyes, engulfed in a blessed darkness.

Ann Davison
Last Voyage

In 1923 W.E. Woodward wrote, 'I am a professional de-bunker'. Since he first used that term the profession has expanded to such an extent that de-bunking has virtually become synonymous with criticism. To imagine that any human being is without clay on his or her boots is to live in cloud cuckoo land. To dwell on the mud and dismiss genuine heroic qualities is equally foolish.

One day when I was feeling very low in spirits I was given a copy of *The Worst Journey in the World*, compiled in the 1920s by Apsley Cherry-Garrard. The book was very much the worse for wear and several pages were missing. The author, drawing on numerous documents, tells the story of Antarctic exploration between the years 1910 and 1913. The stalwart spirit shown by Scott and his companions gave me some strength during miserable times and I have no hesitation in acknowledging my gratitude for the example shown by these courageous individuals.

Monday, March 12. We did 6.9 miles yesterday, under our necessary average. Things are left much the same, Oates not pulling much, and now with hands as well as feet pretty useless. We did 4 miles this morning in 4 hours 20 min – we may hope for 3 this afternoon, $7 \times 6 = 42$. We shall be 47 miles from the depôt. I doubt if we can possibly do it. The surface remains awful, the cold intense, and our physical condition running down. God help us! Not a breath of favourable wind for more than a week, and apparently liable to head winds at any moment.

Wednesday, March 14. No doubt about the going downhill, but everything going wrong for us. Yesterday we woke to a strong northerly wind with temp -37°. Couldn't face it, so remained in camp till 2, then did 5¼ miles. Wanted to march later, but party feeling the cold badly as the breeze (N.) never took off entirely, and as the sun sank the temp. fell. Long time getting supper in dark.

This morning started with southerly breeze, set sail and passed another cairn at good speed: half-way, however, the wind shifted to W. by S. or W.S.W., blew through our wind-clothes and into our mitts. Poor Wilson horribly cold, could [not] get off ski for some time. Bowers and I practically made camp, and when we got into the tent at last we were all deadly cold. Then temp. now mid-day down -43° and the wind strong. We *must* go on, but now the making of every camp must be more difficult and dangerous. It must be near the end, but a pretty merciful end. Poor Oates got it again in the foot. I shudder to think what it will be like tomorrow. It is only with greatest pains rest of us keep off frost-bites. No idea there could be temperatures like this at this time of year with such winds. Truly awful outside the tent. Must fight it out to the last biscuit, but can't reduce rations.

Friday, March 16, or Saturday, 17. Lost track of dates, but think the last correct.

Tragedy all along the line. At lunch, the day before yesterday, poor Titus Oates said he couldn't go on; he proposed we should leave him in his sleeping-bag. That we could not do, and we induced him to come on, on the afternoon march. In spite of its awful nature for him he struggled on and we made a few miles. At night he was worse and we knew the end had come.

Should this be found I want these facts recorded. Oates' last thoughts were of his mother, but immediately before he took pride in thinking that his regiment would be pleased with the bold way in which he met his death. We can testify to his bravery. He has borne intense suffering for weeks without complaint, and to the very last was able and willing to discuss outside subjects. He did not – would not – give up hope till the very end. He was a brave soul. This was the end. He slept through the night before last, hoping not to wake; but he woke in the morning – yesterday. It was blowing a blizzard. He said, 'I am just going outside and may be some time.' He went out into the blizzard and we have not seen him since.

Sunday, March 18. Today, lunch, we are 21 miles the depôt. Ill fortune presses, but better may come. We have had more wind and drift from ahead yesterday; had to stop marching; wind N.W., force 4, temp. -35°. No human being could face it, and we are worn out *nearly*.

My right foot has gone, nearly all the toes – two days ago I was proud possessor of best feet ... Bowers takes first place in condition, but there is not much to choose after all. The others are still confident of getting through – or pretend to be – I don't know. We have the last *half* fill of oil in our primus and a very small quantity of spirit – this alone between us and thirst. The wind is fair for the moment, and that is perhaps a fact to help. The mileage would have seemed ridiculously small on our outward journey.

Monday, March 19. Lunch We camped with difficulty last night and were dreadfully cold till after supper of cold pemmican and biscuit and a half pannikin of cocoa cooked over the spirit. Then, contrary to expectation, we got warm and all slept well. To-day we started in the usual dragging manner. Sledge dreadfully heavy. We are 15½ miles from the depôt and ought to get there in three days. What progress! We have two days' food but barely a day's fuel. All our feet are getting bad – Wilson's best, my right foot worse, left all right. There is no chance to nurse one's feet till we can get hot food into us. Amputation is the least I can hope for now, but will the trouble spread? That is the serious question. The weather doesn't give us a chance – the wind from N. to N.W. and -40° temp. today.

Wednesday, March 21. Got within 11 miles of depôt Monday night; had to lay up all yesterday in severe blizzard. To-day forlorn hope, Wilson and Bowers going to depôt for fuel.

[*March*] *22 and 23.* Blizzard bad as ever – Wilson and Bowers unable to start – to-morrow last chance – no fuel and only one or two of food left – must be near the end. Have decided it shall be natural – we shall march for the depôt with or without our effects and die in our tracks.

Thursday, March 29. Since the 21st we have had a continuous gale from W.S.W. and S.W. We had fuel to make two cups of tea apiece and bare food for two days on the 20th. Every day we have been ready to start for our depôt 11 *miles* away, but outside the door of the tent it remains a scene of whirling drift. I do not think we can hope for any better things now. We shall stick it out to the end, but we are getting weaker, of course, and the end cannot be far.

It seems a pity, but I do not think I can write more.

R. Scott

Last entry For God's sake, look after our people.

The following extracts are from letters written by Scott:

To Mrs. E. A. Wilson

MY DEAR MRS. WILSON, If this letter reaches you, Bill and I will have gone out together. We are very near it now and I should like you to know how splendid he was at the end – everlastingly cheerful and ready to sacrifice himself for others, never a word of blame to me for leading him into this mess. He is suffering, luckily, at least only minor discomforts.

His eyes have a comfortable blue look of hope and his mind is peaceful with the satisfaction of his faith in regarding himself as part of the great scheme of the Almighty. I can do no more to comfort you than to tell you that he died as he lived, a brave, true man – the best of comrades and the staunchest of friends.

My whole heart goes out to you in pity.
Yours,

R. Scott.

To Mrs. Bowers

My dear Mrs Bowers.   I am afraid this
will reach you after one of the heaviest
blows of your life.

I write when we are very near the end of
our journey, and I am finishing it in company with two gallant, noble gentlemen.
One of these is your son. He had come to
be one of my closest and soundest friends,
and I appreciate his wonderful upright
nature, his ability and energy. As the trou-
bles have thickened his dauntless spirit ever
shone brighter and he has remained cheerful, hopeful and indomitable to the end ...

To Sir J. M. Barrie

My dear Barrie.   We are pegging out in
a very comfortless spot. Hoping this letter
may be found and sent to you. I write a

word of farewell ... Good-bye. I am not at all afraid of the end, but sad to miss many a humble pleasure which I had planned for the future on our long marches. I may not have proved a great explorer, but we have done the greatest march ever made and come very near to great success.

Good-bye, my dear friend. Yours ever,

R. SCOTT

We are in a desperate state, feet frozen, etc. No fuel and a long way from food, but it would do your heart good to be in our tent, to hear our songs and the cheery conversation as to what we will do when we get to Hut Point.

Later We are very near the end, but have not and will not lose out good cheer. We have four days of storm in our tent and nowhere's food or fuel. We did intend to finish ourselves when things proved like this, but we have decided to die naturally in the track.

The following extracts are from letters written to other friends:

I want to tell you that I was *not* too old for this job. It was the younger men that went under first ... After all, we are setting a good example to our countrymen, if not by getting into a tight place, by facing it like men when we were there. We could have come through had we neglected the sick.

Wilson, the best fellow that ever stepped, has sacrificed himself again and again to the sick men of the party ...

... Our journey has been the biggest on record, and nothing but the most exceptional hard luck at the end would have caused us to fail to return.

What lots and lots I could tell you of this journey. How much better it has been than lounging in great comfort at home.

Apsley Cherry-Garrard
The Worst Journey in the World

I frequently wished that I could be given an opportunity to talk to my captors about their faith and political philosophy but this was very seldom allowed. Most of the guards who did the routine work had limited English and, even if we had been able to communicate, their grasp of issues was less than informed! The men in higher positions were more articulate but hardly ever discussed such matters with me. It did not surprise me that when they spoke about political questions they did so in terms that were combative. As many people from the so-called 'West' tend to lump all Arabs together, so many Arabs tend to have a uniform distaste for what they perceive as greedy, manipulative, pagan Westerners. One of the leaders told me that he had been to University in the United States and hated all Americans, Germans, British and French. More often than not, hostages were seen as 'symbols' of the pagan West rather than as individuals in their own right. When we were seen as human beings, the natural friendliness of the Arab people broke through.

It soon became clear that my captors were operating as part of a highly structured and disciplined team – not simply a random group of operators: they were subject to strict orders from their superiors and this obviously affected their behaviour towards me.

I lived close to death. In *Taken on Trust* I described the experience of a mock execution when I was told that I had five hours to live. A gun was put to my head and after several moments it was dropped with the words, 'Not now, later'. The building in which I was kept was in the midst of constant shelling and I had several narrow escapes. Towards the end of my captivity, I became ill with a lung infection and, again, death seemed to be at my elbow.

In itself, death did not cause me to be afraid, but I *was* fearful of the way in which I might die. Although I said to myself during a period of serious illness that death would be preferable to what seemed a living death, I did not want to die in captivity. I did not want my family and friends to have to live with the terrible uncertainty of not knowing how I had lived my last days and how I had died. In my work with the families of hostages I had seen too many who had had to experience that particular agony.

When I literally 'felt like death' I would repeat Psalm 23 to myself.

> The Lord is my shepherd: therefore can I
>   lack nothing.
> He shall feed me in a green pasture: and lead
>   me forth beside the waters of comfort.
> He shall convert my soul: and bring me forth
>   in the paths of righteousness, for his
>   Name's sake.
> Yea, though I walk through the valley of the
>   shadow of death, I will fear no evil: for
>   thou art with me; thy rod and thy staff
>   comfort me.
> Thou shalt prepare a table before me against
>   them that trouble me: thou hast
>   anointed my head with oil, and my cup
>   shall be full.

But thy loving-kindness and mercy shall
follow me all the days of my life: and I
will dwell in the house of the Lord for
ever.

The Book of Common Prayer

SOME of my guards told me that death held no fears for them. One mentioned that he had lost his wife in a car bomb incident. Another said that he would be glad to die for his cause as he would then go directly to Paradise.

The way in which we view death will affect the way we live, and vice versa. Whatever we believe, there will always be an element of mystery surrounding this most natural of experiences and I puzzled about it. Death is a certainty and a mystery for us all. It is one reality from which no human being may escape. Harry Williams has expressed something of what I am attempting to say in his book *True Resurrection*:

If we are ready for life in the sense of being open to its power and possibilities, then we are also ready for death. If we are aware of resurrection in the present, then we shall not be over-concerned about resurrection in the future. What Jesus said about becoming as little children and taking no thought for the morrow applies with special force to our future in and beyond the grave. We live now from hour to hour, from minute to minute, as those who are ever receiving from the unknown, and that is all we need to know. Ours can be the confidence of a child living in his father's house whose needs are supplied as, and only as, they arise. Our faith cannot exist in a vacuum of speculative possibilities. Faith is evoked only by the particular situation in which it is needed. (Hence, for example, the impossibility of answering the question, 'Would I be willing to be martyred?') For faith is not a static entity which we have or haven't got or which we have in one degree and not in another. It is always coming into being. It is always being created. It is always being called forth as and when it is needed. When the occasion first arises, we feel as likely as not that our faith is too weak to begin to cope. Then slowly we discover that our faith is matched to our need. And the sign that it is so is seldom any glorious certainty or sense of uplift, but simply the fact that, however much we are wounded and hurt, we are not overwhelmed after all, or perhaps better, being indeed overwhelmed, we still retain that spasmodic glimmer of hope. With regard to all the deaths we have to die, including the final death of the grave, we must always remember that sufficient unto the day is the evil thereof and that as our days are so shall our strength be. If we are like little children we shall not worry about what is going to happen next year or even tomorrow. The source of our confidence cannot be defined. For our confidence is precisely faith in resurrection. And resurrection ceases to be resurrection and becomes no more than another example of human banality, a futile extravaganza, once it is pinned down in a definition. We can experience resurrection at first hand, but we have no concepts, no words, no linguistic forms, in which we can set it out with anything approaching adequacy. We are reminded of Heidegger's statement that 'what is not thought is the supreme gift that any thinking has to give'.

We can approach what is meant only by reading between the lines. For resurrection is God creating, and that passes infinitely beyond the range of our conceptual or linguistic machinery. If we think we have successfully nailed resurrection to the wall, then we are worshipping an idol, and when it is shown up for what it is, we shall feel the need to rush to its defence. 'Divine truth,' on the other hand, 'is a unique kind of uncertainty . . . It comes, if it comes at all, unexpectedly, at some moment of unknowing, exile, abandonment.'*

It must be understood, therefore, that what we have said in this book about resurrection is in terms only of symbols and images which can do no more than point to the reality with which they are concerned. Yet the reality itself is not far off. As our creative source it is nearer to us than we are to ourselves. And if the reality is ultimately indescribable, that is not only because it infinitely transcends us, but also because it encompasses us, informing everything we are as the water informs and fills the sea. For the tabernacle of God is with men as the Eternal Word continuously takes his world to himself and raises it up to resurrection and life.

Harry Williams
True Resurrection

* E. Lampert, in A.J. Philippon (ed.), *The Orthodox Ethos*, Holywell Press, 1964, p. 226.

WHEN Alexander Solzhenitsyn's *The First Circle* found its way to my cell I was delighted because at last I had received a novel of substance. Delighted too because it was a book I had wanted to read again, especially under the circumstances in which I found myself.

The book had been through many hands and for a while I mused on where it had come from and how many people had read it. If a previous owner had written his or her name in a book the guards would generally tear that page out, but sometimes they were careless and would leave it in. I would then stare at the name and wonder about the former reader. This provided a simple link with other people.

The authors of the books I received became very important to me. Some, like Solzhenitsyn, I had met. I pictured them in my mind, recalling what had impressed me on my first meeting. Others, by far the majority, I had never met but I grew to know something of their hopes and desires as I read their books. I wondered if I would ever write a book myself which would find its way across the world.

It was close to Christmas when I read *The First Circle*. I had been alone for several years and was feeling cold and somewhat sad. I read chapter three, in which there is a description of Christmas in prison. I envied the prisoners their companionship.

Two lockers had been pushed up against the stool with the lighted Christmas tree to serve as a table. The six men treated themselves to tinned foods from the *Gastronom* (inmates of special prisons were allowed to order goods from the best stores in Moscow and pay for them out of their earnings), home-made cake, and coffee that was already going cold. A sedate conversation started up, which Max firmly guided towards peaceful subjects: old folk customs, nostalgic stories of Christmas night. Alfred, a bespectacled physics student from Vienna, who had not been able to complete his

studies, spoke with a funny Austrian ac-
cent. Gustav, a youngster from the Hitler
Youth, who had been taken prisoner a week
after the end of the war, sat, round-cheeked,
his pink ears translucent like a piglet's, and
stared wide-eyed at the Christmas lights,
hardly daring to take part in the older men's
conversation.

But they could not keep off the subject
of the war. Someone remembered the
Christmas of 1944, five years before,
when every German had taken pride in
the Ardennes offensive – as in antiquity,
the vanquished had turned the tables on
the victors. They remembered how on that
Christmas Eve Germany had listened to a
speech by Goebbels.

Rubin, plucking at the bristles of his stiff
black beard, said he also remembered that
speech, which had been very telling. Goebbels had spoken with deep anguish, as if he
had personally shouldered the burdens under which Germany was tottering. He

probably already had a premonition of his own end.

SS-Obersturmbannführer Reinhold Simmel, whose long body barely found room between the table and the double bunk, did not appreciate Rubin's tact. He found it unbearable that this Jew should dare to comment on Goebbels at all. He would never have sat down at the same table with him had he had the strength of will to deny himself the company of his compatriots on Christmas Eve. But the other Germans had all insisted on having Rubin. For this handful of Germans, thrown by fate into the golden cage of a special prison in the heart of this bleak and barbarous country, this major from the enemy army, who had spent the whole war spreading discord and destruction among them, was the only man with whom they had a common language. He alone could interpret the local manners and customs for them, advise them how to behave and keep them up to date on what was happening in the world by translating the news from Russian.

Trying his best to needle Rubin, Simmel said that in the Reich there had been plenty of rousing orators and he wondered why the Bolsheviks preferred to read speeches which were prepared and approved in advance.

The remark was all the more wounding for being true. How could one explain the historical reasons for it to this enemy and murderer? Rubin felt nothing but loathing for Simmel. He remembered him when he arrived at Mavrino after many years in Butyrki Prison, still in his creaking leather jacket with the marks on the sleeves where his SS insignia had been ripped off – he had been in the civilian branch, which was by far the worst. Prison had not softened the relentless cruelty of his face, stamped with the mark of Cain. Simmel's presence had made Rubin reluctant to come to this dinner, but the others had been so insistent, and he was so sorry for them in their loneliness that he could not bring himself to cast a shadow on their festivities by staying away.

Trying to keep his temper, Rubin quoted in German Pushkin's advice that certain people should not attempt to deliver judgments higher than their boots.

Max tried to stop tempers rising even more by saying that, with Lev's help, he was beginning to understand Pushkin in the original. He asked Reinhold, why he hadn't taken some whipped cream with his cake, then turned to Lev and asked where he had been that Christmas Eve five years before.

Reinhold helped himself to whipped cream. Lev recalled that five years ago he had been in a bunker by the Narev bridgehead near Rozhan.

And as the five Germans remembered their torn and trampled Germany, decking it out in the richest colours of the mind's eye so too Rubin suddenly thought back to the

Narev bridgehead and the dank forests around Lake Ilmen.

The little coloured lights shone in the six men's eyes. Once again, the Germans asked Rubin to tell them the latest news. But it was embarrassing for him to talk about what had happened in December. He could not play the part of a neutral, a non-Communist, nor could he give up all thought of re-educating these people, but there was no question, either, of explaining to them that in our complex age Socialist truth sometimes progresses in a devious, roundabout way. So he picked out for them, as he did subconsciously for himself, only those current events which showed the main trend, and passed over in silence those which obscured it.

But that particular December nothing positive had taken place, except for the Soviet-Chinese talks – though even they seemed to have got bogged down – and the seventieth birthday of the Leader of the Peoples. He could scarcely tell the Germans about the trial of Traicho Kostov, at which the whole blatant *mise-en-scène* had suddenly come unstuck in open court and the correspondents had been fobbed off, after some delay, with a false confession allegedly written by Kostov in the death cell. This was too shameful, and it would hardly have served the purposes of re-education.

So Rubin dwelt mostly on the historic triumph of the Chinese Communists.

Max listened and nodded agreement, his brown, olive-shaped eyes guileless. He was attached to Rubin, but since the Berlin blockade he had had doubts about the things he told them. Rubin did not know that, in the Microwave Laboratory where he worked, Max at the risk of his neck would occasionally put together a tiny receiver made to look like something else, and then dismantle it. So Max already knew from Cologne and the BBC German service not only about Traicho Kostov – how in court he had repudiated the confession which had been forced out of him during his interrogation – but also about the plans for the North Atlantic Alliance and economic developments in Western Germany. All this, of course, he passed on to the other Germans.

So they just nodded as Rubin spoke.

Actually, it was long past the time for Rubin to go – he had not been let off the whole of the night shift. He said how much he had enjoyed the cake – the student from Vienna gave a little bow of gratification – and began to take his leave. The Germans kept him for as long as politeness required and let him go. Then they started to sing Christmas carols in subdued voices.

Rubin went out into the corridor, carrying a Mongolian dictionary and a volume of Hemingway in English under his arm.

The corridor was wide; it had a temporary floor of rough wood full of splinters. There were no windows, so it was lit day and night by electricity. It was here that, eager for news like the other inmates, Rubin had questioned the prisoners from the camps during the dinner break an hour ago. A door to the main prison staircase opened on this corridor, as did the doors of several cell-like rooms. They were rooms in that they had no locks, but they also qualified as cells because of the peep-holes – little windows in the doors. The peep-holes were never used by the warders but they had been installed, as required by the regulations for ordinary prisons, simply because officially Mavrino counted as a 'Special Prison'.

Alexander Solzhenitsyn
The First Circle

THOSE responsible for getting hold of books must have found the Russian department in the bookshop; when I had finished Solzhenitsyn, the first volume of *The Brothers Karamazov* arrived. It was a Penguin edition and I was annoyed with Penguin for printing this book in two parts for I guessed that I would not see the second volume, and I was right. To receive a book by Dostoyevsky was a wonderful bonus. The sheer power of his writing was a delight and he deals with the great themes: anarchy, atheism, the existence of God and the complexity of the human spirit. It is hard to convey just how much pleasure this book brought to me and now, years later, a Penguin edition of the whole work is open on my desk. It is very difficult indeed to select a passage, and it would be tedious to explain the story. I have taken part of a chapter that held me enthralled: the story of the Grand Inquisitor.

The people weep and kiss the ground upon which he walks. Children scatter flowers before him, sing and cry out to him: 'Hosannah!' 'It is he, it is he himself,' they all repeat. 'It must be he, it can be no one but he.' He stops on the steps of the Cathedral of Seville at the moment when a child's little, open white coffin is brought in with weeping into the church: in it lies a girl of seven, the only daughter of a prominent citizen. The dead child is covered with flowers. 'He will raise up your child', people shout from the crowd to the weeping mother. The canon, who has come out to meet the coffin, looks on perplexed and knits his brows. But presently a cry of the dead child's mother is heard. She throws herself at his feet. 'If it is thou,' she cries, holding out her hands to him, 'then raise my child from the dead!' The funeral cortège halts. The coffin is lowered on to the steps at his feet. He gazes with compassion and his lips once again utter softly the words, 'Talitha cumi' – 'and the damsel arose'. The little girl rises in the coffin, sits up, and looks around her with surprise in her smiling, wide-open eyes. In her hands she holds the nosegay of white roses with which she lay in her coffin. There are cries, sobs, and confusion among the people, and it is at that very moment that the Cardinal himself, the Grand Inquisitor, passes by the cathedral in the square. He is an old man of nearly ninety, tall and erect, with a shrivelled face and sunken eyes, from which, though, a light like a fiery spark still gleams. Oh, he is not wearing his splendid cardinal robes in which he appeared before the people the day before, when the enemies of the Roman faith were being burnt – no, at that moment he is wearing only his old, coarse, monk's cassock. He is followed at a distance by his sombre assistants and his slaves and his 'sacred' guard. He stops in front of the crowd and watches from a distance. He sees everything. He sees the coffin set down at *his* feet, he sees the young girl raised from the dead, and his face darkens. He knits his grey, beetling brows and his eyes flash with an ominous fire. He stretches forth his finger and commands the guards to seize *him*. And so great is his power and so accustomed are the people to obey him, so humble and submissive are they to his will, that the crowd immediately makes way for the guards and, amid the deathlike hush that descends upon the square, they lay hands upon *him* and lead him away. The crowd, like one man, at once bows down to the ground before the old Inquisitor, who blesses them in silence and passes on. The guards take their Prisoner to the dark, narrow, vaulted prison in the old building of the Sacred Court and lock him in there. The day passes and night falls, the dark, hot and 'breathless' Seville night. The air is 'heavy with the scent of laurel and lemon'. Amid the profound darkness, the iron door of the prison is suddenly opened and the old Grand Inquisitor himself slowly enters the prison with a light in his hand.

He is alone and the door at once closes behind him. He stops in the doorway and gazes for a long time, for more than a minute, into his face. At last he approaches him slowly, puts the lamp on the table and says to him:

'Is it you? You?'

Fyodor Dostoyevsky
The Brothers Karamazov

I took my time reading and re-reading *The Brothers Karamazov*. Eventually it was taken from me. Again I thought of the wealth of books available to the world outside and I determined that if I should ever be released I would devote even more time to reading.

Another classic of quite a different order arrived. Arthur Grimble joined the British Colonial Administrative Service and in 1913 received a cadetship in the Gilbert and Ellice Islands Protectorate. I remembered these islands because as a boy their distinctive postage stamps had found a place in my album. Grimble recorded his experiences in a delightful book, *A Pattern of Islands*, and like many other travel books it helped me to escape in my imagination. Later I found a copy on the Cambridge bookstall. Reading the book in captivity brought back a host of memories. My wife Frances and I had lived in Uganda at the end of the Colonial era and, having subsequently travelled throughout the world, I had seen how little Colonial life varied whether one was in the Pacific, Malaysia or Africa.

Grimble was a kindly man, a keen observer and endowed with good common sense. He dedicated his book to the district officers of the Colonial Administrative Service and their long-suffering wives.

I was nominated to a cadetship in the Gilbert and Ellice Islands Protectorate at the end of 1913. The cult of the great god Jingo was as yet far from dead. Most English households of the day took it for granted that nobody could be always right, or ever quite right, except an Englishman. The Almighty was beyond doubt Anglo-Saxon, and the popular conception of Empire resultantly simple. Dominion over palm and pine (or whatever else happened to be noticeably far-flung) was the heaven-conferred privilege of the Bull-dog Breed. Kipling had said so. The colonial possessions, as everyone so frankly called them, were properties to be administered, first and last, for the prestige of the little lazy isle where the trumpet-orchids blew. Kindly administered, naturally – nobody but the most frightful bounder could possibly question our sincerity about that – but firmly too, my boy, firmly too, lest the school-children of Empire forget who were the prefects and who the fags. Your uncles – meaning every man Jack of your father's generation, uncle or not, who cared to take you by the ear – all said you'd never be a leader if you weakened on that point. It was terrifying, the way they put it, for Stalky represented their ideal of dauntless youth, and you loathed Stalky with his Company as much as you feared him; but you were a docile young man, and, as his devotees talked, you felt the seeds of your unworthiness sprouting into shameful view through every crack in your character.

The Colonial Office spoke more guardedly than your uncles. It began by saying that, as a cadet officer, you were going to be on probation for three years. To win confirmation as a member of the permanent administrative staff, you would have to pass within that time certain field-examinations in law and native language. This seemed plain and fair enough, but then came the rider. I forget how it was conveyed, whether in print or by word of mouth; but the gist of it was that you could hardly hope to be taken on as a permanent officer unless, over and above getting through your examinations, you could manage to convince your official chiefs overseas that you possessed qualities of leadership. The abysmal question left haunting you was – did the Colonial Office mean leadership in the same sense as Kipling and your uncles? If it did, and if you were anything like me, you were scuppered.

Arthur Grimble
A Pattern of Islands

ONE of the leading academic institutions in Lebanon is the American University of Beirut. For many years AUB, has provided an education for thousands of young men and women from the Arab world and farther afield. I imagine that one of the reasons I received a good number of books by American writers is that they were left behind by generations of teachers from the University and eventually found their way to second-hand bookshops in the city. A collection of short stories by John Cheever arrived: I was particularly interested in his writings, set in Rome, because he lived there at the same time as Frances and I, and our children went to the same school. This may seem a trivial connection but, in isolation, such small points bring back a flood of memories. Although I had read Cheever, I had not previously read another American writer, William Styron, one of whose books made its way to my cell. *Set this House on Fire* wrestles with the problem of good and evil and held me enthralled. The fact that the book is set in Italy was yet another attraction.

The following extract can give no more than a flavour of the novel.

I barely made it up the hill to Sambuco after leaving Cass and Poppy on the road. It was a murderous climb for my ravaged Austin. After half an hour or so, and a dozen engine-cooling halts along the way, I came in sight of Sambuco's archaic gate: here the car in final mutiny quivered and fulminated and drifted to a stop as the magnificent sea came into view a thousand feet below and as all the trappings of the barbaric valley I had climbed – crags and cliffs and lizard-skittering walls – slipped out of sight behind me. I could hardly believe that I had made it.

Through the archway I could see the piazza of the town, captured in a dazzling noose of sunlight, but the view of the sea from these heights was immediately so theatrical and romantic that it was a few moments before I realized that both town and square seemed oddly quiet and deserted.

It was a stunning view. I stood there for a few seconds hypnotized, once again filled with momentary relief. On the high slope across the valley some wretched poor sheep were grazing, but so perilously and at such a slant that like cutouts pasted there by children, they looked vulnerable to the slightest gust of wind. Then with a sound akin to music and almost beautiful, a bus horn's two fat honking notes floated up from the valley; this and then a church bell far off behind me in the scrubby wilderness made me aware again of how unnaturally silent it was here at the entrance to the town. I trudged off through the dark mildewed archway in search of a telephone, troubled once more, and despairing, and conscious at my sleeve of the quick futile clutch of a hand, of the *carabiniere* in the shadows who whispered to me frantically, much too late: '*Signore, aspett'! C'è il* film!'

I must have only half-heard the cop. At any rate, it pains me still to describe what happened as I strode unheeding past his groping hands, out of the moldering archway, and into the glare of Sambuco's piazza. Submerged in my worries, I must have been so absorbed that I did not notice the fidget and buzz of industry around the café table I blundered into, where sat a man and a woman chattering busily. Here, suddenly and fuzzily bewildered, I tapped the shoulder of a scowling waiter hovering near, my lips parted on the first breath of a question: *Cameriere, per favore, c'è un telefo* . . .

From behind me, I heard someone roar: 'Cut! Cut! Jesus Christ, cut!'

I turned to find myself exposed to a battery of cameras and arc lights and reflectors, and now to the pop-eyed rage of a roly-poly little man in Bermuda shorts bearing down upon me, his lips curled around the butt of a cigar.

'Hey, *paesan*'!' he yelled. 'Vamoose! Get the hell out of here! Umberto, tell this guy to get out of here! He just killed a hundred feet of film! Vamoose out of here, *paesan'*!'

I felt a multitude of eyes upon me – from the mob of townspeople I saw gathered behind ropes gazing on, from the movie folk clustered beneath the lights, especially from the two people at the table I had blundered into. One of them was Carleton Burns, who returned my gaze with his world-famous look of bored, functional disgust. No one laughed. It was like dwelling in an extremely bad dream. For a moment, in the same way that di Lieto's old grandmother had scared me, I felt the queasy visceral terror of a small boy caught at some lurid trespass, and I went weak, cold, and limp and I sensed the blood of pure humiliation knocking at my temples, but then suddenly something in me – perhaps it was the heat, or simply this final embarrassment, or the fact that now, after suffering such conquest all day at the hands of Italy, it was my own countryman, a waddling small blob of one but nevertheless a countryman, who was abusing me – anyway, something within me popped like a valve, and I began to boil over.

'Umberto!' he shouted at me, though not to me. 'Tell that carbinary to keep these people away! Tell this guy to get the hell out of here. Vam – '

'Vamoose yourself, you miserable jerk!' I howled. 'Don't *talk* to me like that! Do I look like an Italian? I've got as much right to this square as you do! Who do you think you are ordering me around – ' In the wilting heat minute orange globes of hysteria exploded before my eyes and I heard my voice bubble up and upward, precariously pitched and rabid but somehow, I knew, almighty, for as I kept shouting at the little man I saw him stop dead in his tracks, cigar butt wagging uncertainly like a semaphore, and with eyes bulging goiterously in indecision and I suspect disbelief.

Of the two final things I remember saying, the first – 'You can't push Italians around!' – seemed as I spoke unscientific and hollow, but a mawkish sense of triumph, the first of the day, swept over me as I yelled, 'I'm a *tired, weary* man!' and on that note turned on my heels and stalked shuddering like a beleaguered and temperamental actor off what, it suddenly occurred to me, was a set.

William Styron
Set this House on Fire

NOVELS by Gore Vidal and John Updike also
found their way to me. Then one day, a small
volume of poetry by Updike arrived. Inside I
came across the following which made me
smile . . .

PLANTING A MAILBOX

Prepare the ground when maple buds have
    burst
And when the daytime moon is sliced so thin
His fibers drink blue sky with litmus thirst.
This moment come, begin.

The site should be within an easy walk,
Beside a road, in stony earth. Your strength
Dictates how deep you delve. The seedling's
    stalk
Should show three feet of length.

Don't harrow, weed, or water; just apply
A little gravel. Sun and motor fumes

Perform the miracle: in late July,
A branch post office blooms.

John Updike

FOR a long time I puzzled about this little poem. It reminded me of something else; but I could not identify it. Then I remembered Virgil and the four books of *The Georgics* dealing with rural life in the first century BC. In the following passage from Book Two, Virgil is instructing his readers in the planting of vines, and I suspect that Updike knew this before he planted his mailbox.

> How to distinguish soils I now will tell you.
> If you want to know whether a soil is light
> Or heavier than most (the one is friendly
> To grain, to grapes the other – heavy to
>   Ceres,
> Light to Lyaeus), first you must select
> A fitting place, then have a pit dug deep
> Into the solid ground. Replace the earth
> And stamp the surface down. If more is
>   needed
> To fill the hole, it's light and fit for pasture
> And genial vines; but if it won't go in

And when the hole is full there's earth to
    spare,
It's heavy: be prepared for clinging clods
And stubborn ridges; plough with sturdy
    oxen.

                Virgil
           The Georgics

IN *Taken on Trust* I told the story of a guard coming into my cell and handing me a postcard of John Bunyan writing in prison. It had been sent to me by a lady from Bedford and was the only mail I received in almost five years. On my release, I told this story and said that I would like to meet the person who had sent the card. I did not make her name public as I wanted the right person to come forward. It so happened that, as I was speaking about the incident during a televised press conference, the lady in question was doing her ironing at home. She nearly dropped the iron when she heard me mention the card. 'Good heavens,' she said to her small daughter, 'that's my card.' Although many thousands of people sent cards and letters, only the card from Mrs Joy Brodier got through. When we met, I was curious to know how she had addressed it because the address had been obliterated when it was given to me. 'Oh,' she said, 'I just sent it to Terry Waite, c/o Hezbollah, Party of God, Lebanon. Unfortunately it was taken from me before I was released.

John Bunyan was imprisoned because he was seen as a threat to both civil and ecclesiastical order. He was a man of considerable spirit, some might say stubborn. I have often mused on the fact that a man imprisoned by the Church of England should bring consolation to an envoy of the Archbishop of Canterbury three hundred years later.

I am including a passage written by Bunyan in which he records his exchange with a visiting Clerk of the Peace. It reveals something of Bunyan's determination.

When I had lain in prison other twelve weeks, and now not knowing what they intended to do with me, upon the 3rd of April 1661, comes Mr Cobb unto me, as he told me, being sent by the justices to admonish me, and demanded of me submittance to the Church of England, etc. The extent of our discourse was as followeth:

COBB. When he was come into the house he sent for me out of my chamber; who, when I was come unto him, he said, Neighbour Bunyan, how do you do?

BUN. I thank you, sir, said I, very well, blessed be the Lord.

COBB. Saith he, I come to tell you that it is desired you would submit yourself to the laws of the land, or else at the next sessions it will go worse with you, even to be sent away out of the nation, or else worse than that.

BUN. I said that I did desire to demean myself in the world, both as becometh a man and a Christian.

COBB. But, saith he, you must submit to the laws of the land, and leave off those meetings which you was wont to have; for the statute law is directly against it; and I am sent to you by the justices to tell you that they do intend to prosecute the law against you if you submit not.

BUN. I said, Sir, I conceive that that law by which I am in prison at this time doth not reach or condemn either me or the meetings which I do frequent. That law was made against those that, being designed to do evil in their meetings, make the exercise of religion their pretence, to cover their wickedness. It doth not forbid the private meetings of those that plainly and simply make it their only end to worship the Lord, and to exhort one another to edification. My end in meeting with others is simply to do as much good as I can, by exhortation and counsel, according to that small measure of light which God hath given me, and not to disturb the peace of the nation.

COBB. Every one will say the same, said he. You see the late insurrection of London, under what glorious pretences they went, and yet, indeed, they intended no less than the ruin of the kingdom and commonwealth.

BUN. That practice of theirs I abhor, said I; yet it doth not follow that, because they did so, therefore all others will do so. I look upon it as my duty to behave myself under the king's government, both as becomes a man and a Christian; and if an occasion were offered me, I should willingly manifest my loyalty to my prince, both by word and deed.

COBB. Well, said he, I do not profess myself to be a man that can dispute; but this I say truly, Neighbour Bunyan, I would have you consider this matter seriously, and submit yourself. You may have your liberty to exhort your neighbour in private discourse, so be you do not call together an assembly of people; and, truly, you may do much good to the Church of Christ, if you would go this way; and this you may do and the law not abridge you of it. It is your private meetings that the law is against.

BUN. Sir, said I, if I may do good to one by my discourse, why may I not do good to two? and if to two, why not to four, and so to eight? etc.

COBB. Ay, saith he, and to a hundred, I warrant you.

BUN. Yes, sir, said I, I think I should not be forbid to do as much good as I can.

COBB. But, saith he, you may but pretend to do good, and indeed, notwithstanding, do harm, by seducing the people; you are therefore denied your meeting so many together, lest you should do harm.

BUN. And yet, said I, you say the law tolerates me to discourse with my neighbour; surely there is no law tolerates me to seduce any one; therefore if I may, by the law, discourse with one, surely it is to do him good, and if I by discoursing may do good to one, surely by the same law I may do good to many.

COBB. The law, saith he, doth expressly forbid your private meetings, therefore they are not to be tolerated.

John Bunyan
The Selected Works

FOR many years I avoided short stories. My dislike could probably be traced back to childhood when I attempted to read some of my father's collection. They bored me to tears. Later, I was introduced to the short stories of Somerset Maugham and realised just how entertaining they could be. I was overjoyed when a volume of Maugham's writings landed in my cell. That was followed by a miscellaneous collection of stories containing one by Stephen Leacock. He was a political scientist in Montreal at McGill University and a writer. One of his shortest stories cheered up a rather depressing day . . .

When I go into a bank I get rattled. The clerks rattle me; the wickets rattle me; the sight of the money rattles me; everything rattles me.

The moment I cross the threshold of a bank and attempt to transact business there, I become an irresponsible idiot.

I knew this beforehand, but my salary had been raised to fifty dollars a month and I felt that the bank was the only place for it.

So I shambled in and looked timidly round at the clerks. I had an idea that a person about to open an account must needs consult the manager.

I went up to a wicket marked 'Accountant'. The accountant was a tall, cool devil. The very sight of him rattled me. My voice was sepulchral.

'Can I see the manager?' I said, and added solemnly, 'alone'. I don't know why I said 'alone.'

'Certainly,' said the accountant, and fetched him.

The manager was a grave, calm man. I held my fifty-six dollars clutched in a crumpled ball in my pocket.

'Are you the manager?' I said. God knows I didn't doubt it.

'Yes,' he said.

'Can I see you,' I asked, 'alone?' I didn't want to say 'alone' again, but without it the thing seemed self-evident.

The manager looked at me in some alarm. He felt that I had an awful secret to reveal.

'Come in here,' he said, and led the way to a private room. He turned the key in the lock.

'We are safe from interruption here,' he said, 'sit down.'

We both sat down and looked at each other. I found no voice to speak.

'You are one of Pinkerton's men, I presume,' he said.

He had gathered from my mysterious manner that I was a detective. I knew what he was thinking, and it made me worse.

'No, not from Pinkerton's,' I said, seeming to imply that I came from a rival agency.

'To tell the truth,' I went on, as if I had been prompted to lie, about it, 'I am not a detective at all. I have come to open an account. I intend to keep all my money in this bank.'

The manager looked relieved but still serious; he concluded now that I was a son of Baron Rothschild or a young Gould.

'A large account, I suppose,' he said.

'Fairly large,' I whispered. 'I propose to deposit fifty-six dollars now and fifty dollars a month regularly.'

The manager got up and opened the door. He called to the accountant.

'Mr Montgomery,' he said unkindly loud, 'this gentleman is opening an account, he will deposit fifty-six dollars. Good morning.'

I rose.

A big iron door stood open at the side of the room.

'Good morning,' I said, and stepped into the safe.

'Come out,' said the manager coldly, and showed me the other way.

I went up to the accountant's wicket and poked the ball of money at him with a quick convulsive movement as if I were doing a conjuring trick.

264

My face was ghastly pale.

'Here,' I said, 'deposit it.' The tone of the words seemed to mean, 'Let us do this painful thing while the fit is on us.'

He took the money and gave it to another clerk.

He made me write the sum on a slip and sign my name in a book. I no longer knew what I was doing. The bank swam before my eyes.

'Is it deposited?' I asked in a hollow, vibrating voice.

'It is,' said the accountant.

'Then I want to draw a cheque.'

My idea was to draw out six dollars of it for present use. Someone gave me a cheque-book through a wicket and someone else began telling me how to write it out. The people in the bank had the impression that I was an invalid millionaire. I wrote something on the cheque and thrust it in at the clerk. He looked at it.

'What! are you drawing it all out again?' he asked in surprise. Then I realised that I had written fifty-six instead of six. I was too far gone to reason now. I had a feeling that it was impossible to explain the thing. All the clerks had stopped writing to look at me.

Reckless with misery, I made a plunge.

'Yes, the whole thing.'

'You withdraw your money from the bank?'

'Every cent of it.'

'Are you not going to deposit any more?' said the clerk, astonished.

'Never.'

An idiot hope struck me that they might think something had insulted me while I was writing the cheque and that I had changed my mind. I made a wretched attempt to look like a man with a fearfully quick temper.

The clerk prepared to pay the money.

'How will you have it?' he said.

'What?'

'How will you have it?'

'Oh' – I caught his meaning and answered without even trying to think – 'in fifties.'

He gave me a fifty-dollar bill.

'And the six?' he asked dryly.

'In sixes,' I said.

He gave it me and I rushed out.

As the big door swung behind me I caught the echo of a roar of laughter that went up to the ceiling of the bank. Since then I bank no more. I keep my money in cash in my trousers pocket and my savings in silver dollars in a sock.

Stephen Leacock
Literary Lapses

I often wondered what the various authors would think if they had known that their books were finding their way to a secret hideout in the Lebanon. I was pleased to find autobiographical details in a book, partly because it helped me to place the writer and also because it provided a small link with another human being.

Several books by Susan Howatch appeared and I identified with her simply because the dust jacket said that she had been born in 1940, the year after me. I had not previously come across her writing, but from the various dust jackets I was able to piece together something of her life.

From reading her novels, I assumed that she had known sorrow and that she was a compassionate woman. I wondered where she was at that moment and whether or not she continued to write. When I was released, I learned that she was indeed still writing, and was in the middle of a series of books centred around the Church of England. This was obviously a new theme and different from the novels I had read.

One day following my release, I was invited to a garden party in Cambridge where another guest was Susan Howatch. She was extremely surprised when I told her my story, and we became friends.

One of her novels, *Glittering Images*, opens in a place I know very well: Lambeth Palace, the London home and office of the Archbishop of Canterbury, where I had my office for many years. She begins her book with a sentence I might have uttered myself . . .

My ordeal began one summer afternoon when I received a telephone call from the Archbishop of Canterbury. It was a hot day, and beyond the window the quadrangle of Laud's shimmered in the hazy light. Term had ended; the resulting peace provided an atmosphere conducive to work, and when the telephone rang it was with reluctance that I reached for the receiver.

A voice announced itself as Lambeth Palace and proclaimed that His Grace wished to speak to Dr Ashworth on a matter of extreme urgency. Apparently the Archbishop was still infecting his chaplains with his love of melodrama.

'My dear Charles!' Dr Lang's voice, always sonorous, now achieved a pitch of theatrical splendour. He was a member of that generation which regards the telephone as at worst a demonic intruder and at best a thespian challenge, and when I inquired diplomatically about his health I was treated to a dramatic discourse on the more tedious aspects of senectitude. The Archbishop, on that first day of July in 1937, was in his seventy-third year and as fit as an ecclesiastical grandee has a right to expect, but in common with all men he hated the manifestations of old age.

' . . . however enough of my tiresome little ailments,' he concluded as I added the finishing touches to the mitre I had sketched on my memo-pad. 'Charles, I'm preaching at Ely next Sunday, and because

I'm most anxious that we should meet I've arranged to spend the night in Cambridge at the house of my old friend the Master of Laud's. I shall come to your rooms after Evensong, but let me stress that I wish my visit to be entirely private. I have a commission which I wish to entrust to you, and the commission,' said the Archbishop, milking the situation of every ounce of drama by allowing his voice to sink to a whisper, 'is very delicate indeed.'

I wondered if he imagined he could arrive at my rooms without being recognized. Archbishops hardly find it easy to travel incognito, and an archbishop who had recently played a leading part in the abdication of one king and the coronation of another was hardly the most anonymous of clerics.

I said politely, 'Of course I'd be glad to help you in any way I can, Your Grace.'

'Then I'll see you on Sunday evening. Thank you, Charles,' said Dr Lang, and after giving me a brisk blessing he terminated the call. I was left staring at the mitre I had sketched, but gradually I became aware that my gaze had shifted to the last words I had written before the interruption.

'Modalism appealed to the Church's desire for monotheism, but in the second half of the fourth century it was propounded that the modalist God metamorphosed himself to meet – '

The impact of Modalism on the doctrine of the Trinity seemed a long way from the machinations of Dr Lang.

I found I had lost interest in my new book.

My ordeal had begun.

Susan Howatch
Glittering Images

THE stockpile of books collected by the guards was beginning to run out and it was with increasing insistence that they told me to 'read slow'. I received *Count Belisarius* by Robert Graves and enjoyed it enormously. Then, to my surprise a translation of *The Odyssey* arrived to be followed by James Joyce. I had hoped to receive *Ulysses*, which I had only partially read and I longed to receive books that would make demands on me. It was, however, one of Joyce's shorter works that arrived: *Dubliners*.

Some people regard Joyce as being virtually inaccessible, but this is far from true. *Dubliners*, an account of the lives of ordinary men and women, reveals the extraordinary talent of the author. As he recounts the everyday happenings of his characters, he conveys, with the greatest subtlety, the fragile web of emotions that lie but a fraction beneath the surface of events.

One of the most enjoyable stories from *Dubliners* is entitled 'The Dead'. I read it time and again. There is only space here to include a part of this picture painted by a master of language.

It is Christmas in Dublin and the Misses Morkan have gathered with their friends for a Christmas celebration. The following extract gives a flavour of the conversation around the dining table. Mr Browne is, of course, 'of the other persuasion' namely, a Protestant.

The clatter of forks and spoons began again. Gabriel's wife served out spoonfuls of the pudding and passed the plates down the table. Midway down they were held up by Mary Jane, who replenished them with raspberry or orange jelly or with blanc-mange and jam. The pudding was of Aunt Julia's making, and she received praises for it from all quarters. She herself said that it was not quite brown enough.

'Well, I hope, Miss Morkan,' said Mr Browne, 'that I'm brown enough for you because, you know, I'm all Brown.'

All the gentlemen, except Gabriel, ate

some of the pudding out of compliment to Aunt Julia. As Gabriel never ate sweets the celery had been left for him. Freddy Malins also took a stalk of celery and ate it with his pudding. He had been told that celery was a capital thing for the blood and he was just then under doctor's care. Mrs Malins, who had been silent all through the supper, said that her son was going down to Mount Melleray in a week or so. The table then spoke of Mount Melleray, how bracing the air was down there, how hospitable the monks were and how they never asked for a penny-piece from their guests.

'And do you mean to say,' asked Mr Browne incredulously, 'that a chap can go down there and put up there as if it were a hotel and live on the fat of the land and then come away without paying anything?'

'O, most people give some donation to the monastery when they leave,' said Mary Jane.

'I wish we had an institution like that in our Church,' said Mr Browne candidly.

He was astonished to hear that the monks never spoke, got up at two in the morning and slept in their coffins. He asked what they did it for.

'That's the rule of the order,' said Aunt Kate firmly.

'Yes, but why?' asked Mr Browne.

Aunt Kate repeated that it was the rule, that was all. Mr Browne still seemed not to understand. Freddy Malins explained to him, as best he could, that the monks were trying to make up for the sins committed by all the sinners in the outside world. The explanation was not very clear, for Mr Browne grinned and said:

'I like that idea very much, but wouldn't a comfortable spring bed do them as well as a coffin?'

'The coffin,' said Mary Jane, 'is to remind them of their last end.'

As the subject had grown lugubrious it was buried in a silence of the table, during which Mrs Malins could be heard saying to her neighbour in an indistinct undertone:

'They are very good men, the monks, very pious men.'

James Joyce
Dubliners

AFTER almost four years, a day that I had been dreading arrived: there were no more books. I asked to receive back some of the volumes I had read previously but was told that they were irretrievable. I imagined they had been given to other captives elsewhere. Now, once again, I was left totally alone with memory.

The longer my solitary state lasted, the more I appreciated the harmony and rhythm of language. In solitary confinement the individual is afraid of losing inner coherence, and the rhythm of language assists inner balance. Music, had that been available, would have fulfilled a similar function. Years before I had asked one of the guards to bring me Shakespeare and he had made a special effort to be helpful. To my sadness he brought only *Lamb's Tales from Shakespeare*. That was the nearest the Bard ever got to my cell. I remembered fragments from schooldays but not enough to be satisfying.

My health began to fail as I choked on fumes entering my room from a generator situated on the balcony outside. It was winter and very cold. I was ill and probably near to death. Someone once described death as the ultimate reality. I thought of Von Hügel who said:

> The deeper we get into reality,
> the more numerous will be
> the questions we cannot answer

One Christmas Eve, wrapped in my blanket, I said the Communion Service to myself and recited the first Chapter of the Gospel of St John.

The word, spoken of by the writer, is the Divine Word, the Logos, the eternal truth for which we seek. Truth that was, and is, and shall be for ever. A mystery . . .

> In the beginning was the Word, and the Word was with God, and the Word was God.
> The same was in the beginning with God.
> All things were made by him; and without him was not any thing made that was made.

In him was life; and the life was the light of men.

And the light shineth in darkness; and the darkness comprehended it not.

There was a man sent from God, whose name was John.

The same came for a witness, to bear witness of the Light, that all men through him might believe.

He was not that Light, but was sent to bear witness of that Light.

That was the true Light, which lighteth every man that cometh into the world.

He was in the world, and the world was made by him, and the world knew him not.

He came unto his own, and his own received him not.

But as many as received him, to them gave he power to become the sons of God, even to them that believe on his name:

Which were born, not of blood, nor of the
will of the flesh, nor of the will of man,
but of God.

And the Word was made flesh, and dwelt
among us, (and we beheld his glory, the
glory as of the only begotten of the
Father,) full of grace and truth.

John 1:1–14

THE words of an Italian poem translated by Ezra Pound echoed in my mind:

> When the light
> goes, men shut behind blinds their life, to die
>   for a night.
>
> And yet
> through glass and bars
> some dream a wild sunset
> waiting the stars.
>
> Call these few, at least
> the singers, in whom
> hope's voice is yeast.

During the four years of exile and solitude, I had attempted to hold to the light. At times my grasp was feeble, but hope never totally died. The authority on world religions, Mircea Eliade, in his published notebooks, *No Souvenirs*, wrote about exile and the path towards the centre. I recognised that my solitude had been an exile of a kind.

'Every real existence' he said, 'reproduces the *Odyssey*.' The chance to become a new Ulysses is given to *any* exile *whomsoever* . . . to realise this, the exile must be capable of penetrating the hidden meaning of his wanderings and of understanding them as a long series of initiation trials, and as so many obstacles on the path which brings him back to the hearth (the centre). That means seeing signs, hidden meanings, symbols, in the sufferings, the depressions, the dry periods in everyday life. Seeing them and reading them even *if they aren't there*; if one sees them, one can build a structure and read a message in the formless flow of things and the monotonous flux of historical facts.'

Across the years the words of many men and women had come to me through books. They had made me laugh, cry, rejoice and enabled me to maintain some sense of perspective. They had also assisted me as I attempted to give meaning to my own myth, my own journey which, for a space, was concentrated on discovering the centre. When the exploration became too exhausting they provided me with a little human companionship.

My faith enabled me to interpret experience and give meaning to that which might have seemed meaningless.

In the final part of his autobiography, Stephen Spender touches on many of my own thoughts.

In the dormitory, in the watches of the night, I thought that one day I would write a book which would contain the truth to which I bore witness. What I would say was perfectly clear to me. It was this: everyone is occupied in blindly pursuing his own ends, and yet beneath his aims, and beneath his attempts to escape from solitude by conforming with the herdlike behaviour of those around him, he wants something quite different from his aims, and quite different from the standards of human institutions, and this thing which he wants is what all want: simply to admit that he is an isolated existence, and that his class and nation, even the personality and character which he presents to his fellow beings, are all a mask, and beneath this mask there is only the desire to love and be loved just because he is ignorant, and miserable, and surrounded by unknowns of time and space and other people.

In the night of my childhood, I saw that the smallness and brevity of a human life, compared with the infinitude of time and the immensity of the universe, dwarf each separate person, and the most the cleverest can know is that he knows nothing. Within each there is a world of his own soul as immense as the external universe, and equally with that, dwarfing the little stretch of coherent waking which calls itself 'I'.

Standing midway between vast interior and exterior natures, each one is equal with the others, in enclosing within his own littleness a spark of consciousness of all.

He does not even know himself or others, so that he can never even say with conviction: 'I am better than the others'; and yet, alas, he knows enough to be able to think: I am worse.'

All men know is that conditioning in time and space and human psychology which all share in common, and which throw them into life like shipwrecked people upon a sea. In their situation the only sanity must lie in helping one another, and above all for each generation, to remember that the New World is simply their children, who form the next.

Undoubtedly certain old poems, certain texts, certain laws even, said all this with sacred authority: to hear them, as I lay awake, was like seeing cold water falling through the night which had the power to wash and shape the stone which was my heart. When I read of the lives of those saints of utterly simple purpose who had put aside all evasion and lived for humanity, making their own material welfare the lowest common multiple of the material existence of the poor, I felt a deep obeisance of my nature, and I knew that their illogicality was right.

So I thought that under all causes and all appearances, there was an extreme simplicity, like that of a lost child or a sick person. What really mattered were extreme situations, in the light of which ordinary ones should be judged: the beginning of creation, the end of the world, extreme poverty or suffering, great love, death. Life acquired significance – I thought, when I was nine or ten – in so far as isolated moments of living were stretched upon these extremes, penetrated by the awareness of ultimate ends. Health and well-being and comfort should not simply be an escape into the body or the money from the realities which are always present, and which all finally have to face.

Of course these ideas were childish, and when I thought that I would one day write a book which stated them very simply, I was a child. Yet now I am a middle-aged man, in the centre of life and rotted by a modicum of success, surrounded on the one hand by material responsibilities and on the other by material achievements, it seems to me that the boy I was, was aware of the dangers I have fallen into now – for didn't I read in many legends of purposes forgotten, of forests full of thorns, of grails unnoticed? My mistake was to think that my own nature would make everything easy. Perhaps I was less a child when the purpose was clearer, and now that I am old I am encumbered by many childish things. Yet the fact remains that I am and was the same person: when I was a child there were moments when I stood up within my whole life, as though it were a burning room, or as though I were rowing alone on a sea whose waves were filled with many small tongues of fire: and where I thought of my son, and my daughter, and my ancestors, and when I remembered how my mother, the night before she died, said to Ella, who was lighting the little gas fire in her bedroom, 'Tell them I have had a very happy life.'

(1947 – May 30 1950)

Stephen Spender
World within World

ON my release there were many good friends who gave both my family and I solid support. One such was Francis Witts. Francis has another incidental link with this book and in his youth he travelled with Freya Stark.

Francis's great-great-grandfather, The Revd. F.E. Witts, was Rector of Upper Slaughter in Gloucestershire. He is chiefly remembered because for every day of his adult life he kept a diary. These journals, written in the first half of the nineteenth century, give a unique insight into Gloucestershire life of that period. They were carefully preserved by the Witts family and in the last years Francis has made them available for publication.

The entry dated 22 August 1838 gives an amusing account of how Parson Witts viewed his bishop.

August 22nd, 1832
The Bishop arrived at the Unicorn Inn at Stow from Campden, where he had

confirmed and visited yesterday, complaining of fatigue and over-exertion and suffering from the increased infirmity of his eyesight. He received me with his wonted friendship. When His Lordship had robed, he went to the church, where confirmation was administered to, I suppose, nearly 400 young persons of both sexes. All was done with much order and decorum. The Bishop delivered a suitable, plain but rather feeble and commonplace discourse on confirmation. The Bishop and clergy retired for an hour to the Rectory. Several ladies were present; Mrs. Leigh of Stoneleigh Abbey with a daughter who has been confirmed. My son and daughter who were greeted by Bishop Monk with the utmost cordiality and kindness. At 2 o'clock we returned to the church for evening service. The Bishop's charge was very long and laboured; his imperfect vision led to much hesitation ... his unwillingness to exhaust the attention of his hearers led him to curtail his charge by

omitting considerable portions, and consequently the line or argument was interrupted.

Bishop Monk is a man of very kindly
disposition very well meaning; but lacks
judgement, and is of a very susceptible,
irritable, and sensitive temeperament. The
evening exceedingly damp and cold; but the
labours of the day not yet over as we sallied
forth in our chariot to meet the Bishop at
Mr. Ford's (at Little Rissington) where he
was to sleep preparatory to two Confirma-
tions fixed for to-morrow at Bourton-on-
the-Water and Northleach. The Bishop
adverted to a subject of some local importance as regards his now greatly extended
diocese, in which there are no less that three
charitable associations for affording pecuni-
ary relief to distressed clergymen, their
widows and orphans; that long established
in the old diocese of Gloucester, a like
association for the City of Bristol, and a
third in North Wiltshire. The Bishop

thinks it desirable that these should be concentrated into one; but it is obvious that such an arrangement will be fraught with many difficulties.

David Verey, ed.
The Diary of a Cotswold Parson

RECENTLY, when I was speaking at a public function, my audience was anxious to hear about solitary confinement and I attempted to answer questions. One man got to his feet and half apologised for this comment:

'I don't want to belittle what you have been through,' he said, 'but in some ways you have been fortunate. You have been given an opportunity to evaluate your life and go more deeply into inner experience. Most of us are so busy trying to make a living that we never get the chance to reflect.'

I assured him that his apology was unnecessary because there was a great deal of truth in what he said. My captivity was certainly a miserable experience which I would not wish to go through again. And yet, almost despite myself, something had come from it.

When the manuscript of this book was completed in draft, my editor pointed out that I had chosen a number of accounts of journeys. I believe that journeys fascinated me not only because I longed to travel away from my cell but also because I was conscious of the fact that I was in the midst of a unique inner journey. If I have not fully described this here it is perhaps because I am still attempting to interpret the landscape. There are many questions I cannot begin to answer, nor even to frame. I know that I was able to take the experience of captivity and turn it into something creative. There was a cost, a high and painful cost, and at times the pain lingers. There have been benefits. I have learnt to embrace solitude as a friend and I no longer experience that aching loneliness which made me such a compulsive individual. I have long appreciated the beauty of form and order in life, but I no longer feel so insecure that I have to be dogmatic to the point of arrogance. I now understand *in my inner experience* what Eliot was communicating when he wrote:

We shall not cease from exploration
And the end of our exploring

Will be to arrive where we started
And know the place for the first time.*

As a child I was so conscious of the mystery of
the universe and the wonder of life. I have
returned to that place and the return has
brought me to realise anew that all true faith
should at least enable us to touch the hem of
mystery.

I remember asking myself a question in
captivity. If I ever regained my freedom what
should I wish to do with the remainder of my
life? I gave four answers. To give more time to
reading and meditation; to write; to engage in
public speaking and, finally, to continue with the
humanitarian activities which have concerned
me throughout my life. I have put the answers
in this order because I have learnt that worth-
while action springs from a centre that is aware,
still; and yet, not without tension.

Like Stephen Spender, I understand the attraction and seeming illogicality of simplicity. I

* T.S. Eliot, 'Little Gidding' from *The Four Quartets*

do not agree when he says his ideas were 'childish'. I believe they were 'childlike'. There is a difference between the two. My own journey through life has been greatly enhanced by the intensity of the experience of captivity, but I am deeply aware of the fact that there is still a long way to tread. The goal? Wholeness – a concept that cannot be realised selfishly.

Stephen Spender expresses something of the difficulties of the journey in his poem 'Darkness and Light'.

> To break out of the chaos of my darkness
> Into a lucid day, is all my will.
> My words like eyes in night, stare to reach
> A centre for their light: and my acts thrown
> To distant places by impatient violence
> Yet lock together to mould a path
> Out of my darkness, into a lucid day.
>
> Yet, equally, to avoid that lucid day
> And to preserve my darkness, is all my will.
> My words like eyes that flinch from light,
> refuse

And shut upon obscurity; my acts
Cast to their opposites by impatient violence
Break up the sequent path; they fly
On a circumference to avoid the centre.

To break out of my darkness towards the centre
Illumines my own weakness, when I fail;
The iron arc of the avoiding journey
Curves back upon my weakness at the end;
Whether the faint light spark against my face
Or in the dark my sight hide from my sight,
Centre and circumference are both my
     weakness.

O strange identity of my will and weakness!
Terrible wave white with the seething word!
Terrible flight through the revolving darkness!
Dreaded light that hunts my profile!
Dreaded night covering me in fears!
My will behind my weakness silhouettes
My territories of fear, with a great sun.

I grow towards the acceptance of that sun
Which hews the day from night. The light

Runs from the dark, the dark from light
Towards a black and white total emptiness.
The world, my life, binds the dark and light
Together, reconciles and separates
In lucid day the chaos of my darkness.

Stephen Spender
The Still Centre

I am writing these lines during the week before Easter when the Church reflects on the great cyclical process of birth, death and resurrection. This theme contains truths which we know to be self-evident. We are born into this world and we shall die. Spring, summer, seedtime, harvest: the pattern of death and resurrection runs through the whole of life. The world, of which we are a part, replenishes itself. The process of creation is ongoing and we are active, though perhaps not always conscious, participants in that process.

To believe in resurrection requires faith, and even faith is a natural part of human experience. Those who have applied their faith are fortunate, if not always comfortable. They are fortunate because they will look forward to resurrection, but more – they will know something of it within their own experience.

They will never be totally comfortable, for faith must point to truth and truth always disturbs as it heals. Whether we have religious faith or not, we are linked together on a journey through life – a journey that may take us into the very depths of suffering as well as to the heights of joy.

I should like to close this part of the journey with the words of a very old prayer: a collect. The word simply means a 'gathering together', and this prayer has brought together people of faith for over fifteen hundred years. It is a gentle request composed by a bishop of Rome in AD 492.

Almighty and everlasting God, who,
of thy tender love towards mankind,
hath sent thy Son, our Saviour Jesus Christ,
to take upon him our flesh and to suffer
death upon the cross,
that all mankind should follow the example
of his great humility: Mercifully grant,
that we may both follow the example of
his patience,
and also be made partakers of his
resurrection;
though the same Jesus Christ our Lord.
Amen.

INDEX OF SOURCES

Sources are listed in text order

T.S. Eliot, 'Burnt Norton' from *The Four Quartets* (Faber & Faber).

G. Bramwell Evens, *A Romany in the Fields* (The Epworth Press, 1929), pp. 26–8.

Nicholas Tucker, *The Child and the Book* (CUP, 1981; Canto, 1990), pp. 120–1.

J.M. Cohen (ed.), *The Penguin Book of Comic and Curious Verse* (Penguin, 1952), p. 32.

Arthur Ransome, *Swallows and Amazons* (Cape, 1930; Puffin, 1962), pp. 31–3.

Freya Stark, *Beyond Euphrates* (Murray, 1951; Century Hutchinson, 1983) pp. 4–5.

'General Confession', *The Book of Common Prayer*.

'Psalm 121', *The Book of Common Prayer*.

Hubert Northcott CR, *The Venture of Prayer* (SPCK, 1950), p. 172.

G.H. Hardy, *A Mathematician's Apology* (CUP, 1940; Canto, 1992), pp. 63–6.

'Address to Shakespeare', *The Complete McGonagall* (Duckworth, 1980).

Lord Byron, *The Prisoner of Chillon* from *Poetical Works* (Oxford, 1904), p. 340.

A.L. Rowse, 'In the Train to Cambridge' from *A Life – Collected Poems* (William Blackwood, 1981).

Fred D'Aguiar, *The Longest Memory* (Chatto & Windus, 1994), prelims, unpaginated.

Gavin Young, *Slow Boat Home* (Hutchinson, 1985, Penguin, 1986), pp. 418–20.

J.M. Rodwell (tr), *The Koran* (J.M. Dent Everyman Series, 1909, 1953), pp. ix–x.

M.M. Pickthall (tr), *The Koran* (The Islamic Call Society, Tripoli).

Arthur Koestler, *Darkness at Noon* (Cape), pp. 47–51.

Eric Newby, *A Traveller's Life* (Collins, 1982), pp. 221–3.

Betty Smith, *A Tree Grows in Brooklyn* (Mandarin, 1992), pp. 136–7.

Alistair Cooke, *Talk About America* (Knopf, 1968), pp. 146–8.

Marcus Aurelius, *Meditations* (J.M. Dent Everyman Series, 1961), tr A.S.L. Farquharson (Clarendon Press), pp. 64–5.

Dorothy L. Sayers, *Busman's Honeymoon* (Gollancz, 1937; Hodder & Stoughton, 1988), pp. 102–4.

Michael Innes, *Appleby's End* (Gollancz, 1946, Penguin, 1969), pp. 7–9.

C.G. Jung, *Memories, Dreams, Reflections* (Collins and RKP, 1963; Fount, 1977), tr Richard and Clara Winston, pp. 7, 17–19.

Bede Griffiths, *Return to the Centre* (Collins, 1976), pp. 17–18.

Carlo Carretto, *Letters from the Desert* (Darton, Longman & Todd, 1972) pp. 137–8.

Evelyn Waugh, 'Remote People' from *When the Going was Good* (Penguin, 1951), pp. 103–5.

Alan Moorhead, *The Blue Nile* (The Reprint Society, 1963), pp. 236–8.

The Letters of Queen Victoria, Second Series (John Murray, 1926), pp. 417–19.

Herodotus, *History of the Greek and Persian War* (1st pub. c. 430 BC; New English Library, 1966), pp. 88–9.

Timothy Ware, *The Orthodox Church* (Pelican Original, 1963), pp. 206–7.

Irina Ratushinskaya, *Grey is the Colour of Hope* (Hodder & Stoughton, 1988; Seahorse Inc), tr © Alyona Kojevnikov, pp. 29–30.

An Interrupted Life. The Diaries of Etty Hillesum (Pantheon, Eng. tr Jonathan Cape, 1983), pp. 81–2.

Desmond Tutu, *Hope and Suffering* (Scotaville Pubrs, Johannesburg, 1983; Collins Fount), pp. 170–2, 174.

Laurie Lee, *As I Walked out one Midsummer Morning* (Andre Deutsch, 1969; Penguin, 1971), pp. 112–14.

Ann Davison, *Last Voyage* (Peter Davies, 1951; Pan Paperback, 1956), pp. 214–16.

Apsley Cherry-Garrard, *The Worst Journey in the World*, 2 vols (Penguin, 1937), pp. 526–7, 627–30.

'Psalm 23', *The Book of Common Prayer*.

H.A. Williams, *True Resurrection* (Mitchell Beazley, London, 1972), pp. 180–1.

Alexander Solzhenitsyn, *The First Circle* (Collins, 1968), pp. 22–6

Fyodor Dostoyevsky, *The Brothers Karamazov* (Penguin Classics, 1958), pp. 292–4.

Arthur Grimble, *A Pattern of Islands* (John Murray, 1952), pp. 1–2.

William Styron, *Set this House on Fire* (© 1959, 1960 William Styron; Hamish Hamilton, 1961, Black Swan, Transworld, 1985), pp. 68–70.

John Updike, *Collected Poems* (Alfred Knopf, 1993; Hamish Hamilton, UK, 1993; Penguin, 1995), p. 292.

Virgil, *The Georgics* (Penguin Classics, 1982), Bk 2, p. 84.

John Bunyan, *The Selected Works*, pp. 696–8.

Stephen Leacock, *Literary Lapses* (1910; Penguin, 1939), pp. 7–10.

Susan Howatch, *Glittering Images* (Collins, 1987), pp. 3–4.

James Joyce, *Dubliners* (1914; Cape, 1967; Mandarin, 1992), pp. 280–1.

'The Gospel According to St John', King James Version of The Bible (CUP), vv. 1–14.

Ezra Pound, 'When the light goes' from *Translations* (Faber and Faber, 1953).

Mircea Eliade, *No Souvenirs* (Gallimard, 1973; RKP, 1978).

Stephen Spender, autobiography, *World Within World* (Hamish Hamilton, 1951), pp. 334–6

David Verey, ed., *The Diary of a Cotswold Parson* (Allan Sutton Publishing, Phoenix Mill, Stroud, Gloucestershire), p.150.

FOOTFALLS IN MEMORY

T.S. Eliot, 'Little Gidding' from *The Four Quartets* (Faber & Faber).

Stephen Spender, 'Darkness and Light', *The Still Centre* (1935).